Praise for
Unlocking Your Parish

"This excellent book provides a very practical and inspiring account of the impact Alpha has had in forming missionary disciples at Saint Benedict Parish, Canada. Ron Huntley and Fr. James Mallon share their experience and wisdom with a passion that is both engaging and compelling. I highly recommend *Unlocking Your Parish*."

—**Nicky Gumbel,** Vicar of Holy Trinity Brompton, London and pioneer of Alpha

"Jesus said you judge a tree by its fruit. Mallon and Huntley's experience is mine: Alpha, used as a tool, a part of a larger strategy for parish renewal, is hands down the best thing I've seen for leading people into a life-changing encounter with Jesus."

—**Fr. John Riccardo,** Pastor, Our Lady of Good Counsel Parish, Plymouth, Michigan

"*Unlocking Your Parish* is a goldmine of practical wisdom for transforming a parish into a community of missionary disciples. Drawing on years of experience, Ron Huntley and Fr. James Mallon explain why Alpha is a powerful tool for evangelization and how to navigate the challenges involved in changing a parish culture. Together they consider the full spectrum of questions—from the appropriateness of Alpha in a Catholic setting to how to choose an Alpha emcee. From beginning to end, this book is engaging, inspiring, and challenging to our preconceived ideas about parish renewal. I will be recommending it everywhere I go!"

—**Dr. Mary Healy**, Professor of Sacred Scripture, Sacred Heart Major Seminary

"For the last few years, as the pastor of multiple parishes, each with a with different culture and history, I've been challenged by Pope Francis to create a common space for a 'renewed personal encounter with Christ.' Alpha has been for us one of the greatest tools in bringing people together and, even more importantly, focusing us on making disciples. *Unlocking your Parish* offers great wisdom about building a culture of encounter through Alpha. Using their own prayerful experiences and passionate hearts, Fr. Mallon and Ron also share practical insights: pitfalls to avoid, along with simple steps to help plan, start, maintain, and grow Alpha as a tool to raise up leaders and create an outward-focused community intentional about making disciples. Truly a blessing."

—**Rev. Msgr. Robert J. Jaskot,** Pastor, Pastorate of Saint Francis-Saint Mary and Holy Family, Maryland

"This book is essential for any Catholic parish considering Alpha. As I read it I kept saying to myself, 'I wish I had had this book five years ago when we started our Alpha journey!' But God's timing is perfect and he has generously placed this book in my hands just as we are starting to realize how Alpha fits into the overall strategy and vision for evangelization and discipleship in our parish. Thank you, Ron Huntley and Fr. Mallon, for this amazing guide filled with practical steps and encouragement."

—**Anne Cook,** Coordinator of Adult Formation and Evangelization, St. Joseph Catholic Church, Marblehead, Ohio

"You will want to make room on your bookshelf for this timely resource if you are passionate about the Great Commission and serious about parish renewal. Fr. James Mallon and Ron Huntley have gifted the Church with an important book seasoned with experience, wisdom, and practical advice, answering common questions many have about Alpha and its extraordinary potential to transform lives and parishes. Whether you're new to Alpha or running your hundredth Alpha, I highly recommend this insightful work."

—**Mary Guilfoyle**, Evangelization and Discipleship Director, Our Lady of Good Counsel Parish and Alpha USA Hub Director

"After serving in sixteen Spanish-speaking Alpha sessions (so far) as a helper, cohost, host, and session leader I have seen how Alpha has helped form new friendships, restore families, and inspire participants to serve in ministry with a new heart. *Unlocking Your Parish* answered all the questions and concerns I have had while being involved with Alpha. I am forever grateful to Fr. Mallon and Ron Huntley for this gift."

—**Suling Cheaz-Laposa**, Alpha Session Leader-Spanish, St. Ann Catholic Parish, Coppell, Texas

Ron Huntley works internationally with church leaders to build passion and get results. Ron's love for Jesus, people, and the church drive him to make a difference in the lives of pastors, priests, and ministry leaders everywhere. Ron Huntley and Fr. James Mallon worked side by side to bring about the Divine Renovation at Saint Benedict Parish in Halifax, Canada. Ron's work has expanded to parishes around the world through international speaking engagements, the Divine Renovation podcast, and the Divine Renovation leadership coaching network, through which he raises up and supports coaches, and mentors pastors who seek to bring their parish from maintenance to mission.

Fr. James Mallon is the part-time Episcopal Vicar for Parish Renewal and Leadership Support for the Archdiocese of Halifax-Yarmouth, Nova Scotia, Canada. Although now former pastor of Saint Benedict Parish in Halifax, he is still very much part of the faith community.

Fr. James is the author of the bestselling book *Divine Renovation: Bringing Your Parish from Maintenance to Mission* and the *Divine Renovation Guidebook*.

The message of Divine Renovation has resonated in the hearts of tens of thousands of pastors and the laity throughout the world. To answer their needs, the Divine Renovation Ministry was created. Fr. James serves the Archdiocese with half of his time and serves in the Divine Renovation Ministry with the other half of his time.

We would like to thank Deacon Keith Strohm for his support in bringing this book to completion.

Divine
Renovation

Unlocking
Your Parish

Making Disciples,
Raising Up Leaders with Alpha

Ron Huntley & Fr. James Mallon

theWORD
among us®
Press

Published by The Word Among Us Press
7115 Guilford Drive, Suite 100
Frederick, Maryland 21704
wau.org

23 22 21 20 19   1 2 3 4 5

ISBN: 978-1-59325-365-3
eISBN: 978-1-59325-535-0

Cover design by Faceout Studios

Made and printed in the United States of America

Library of Congress Control Number: 2018958980

Contents

Introduction

RON HUNTLEY

I'm passionate about parish transformation. I'm passionate about it because transformed parishes transform people, and transformed people transform the world around them.

This work of parish transformation requires us to change parish culture—starting with choosing a mission-oriented over a maintenance-oriented culture—that is, the organizational structure and the this-is-the-way-we've-always-done-things thinking that can make change difficult. Parish transformation requires moving beyond a maintenance-oriented culture in which our concern is restricted to caring for the flock—the parishioners. Instead, transformation requires that we choose a mission-oriented culture in which the parish, while caring for the flock, is mobilized to turn outwards to reach those on the outside. That's hard work.

When I come alongside parishes to coach their leaders, I talk about three important elements of a healthy parish: the soil, the seed, and the fruit. Now, we all want to see fruit. We all want to see lives changed by Jesus and for our communities to become effective channels of his love for the world. So what do we do? We get some good seeds—in other words, the best programs—and expect them to bear the fruit we're looking for.

We forget, though, the critical role of the soil. That soil is the culture of our parishes. Even the best seeds cannot develop fruit when they are planted in barren or toxic soil. Changing the culture of our parishes to make them healthier and more life-giving enriches the soil so that we can bear "fruit that will remain" (John 15:16).

Within Divine Renovation Ministry, we have a Divine Renovation Network through which we coach parishes around the world. We have discovered, in our work, that one of the most effective tools for changing culture and sparking transformation is Alpha, a multi-week process that encompasses the proclamation of the gospel message and relationship building.

Alpha is a parish tool for evangelization based on hospitality, sharing, and open conversation. The same Alpha content is run all over the world, by Christians of all traditions, and provides a common expression of proclamation, service, and witness. Millions of people have experienced Alpha in over one hundred countries and over one hundred languages around the globe. Alpha sessions include a good meal, an engaging movie, and casual conversation in a small group setting. Developed out of an Anglican parish in London, England, Alpha offers an opportunity to explore the meaning of life and to receive a basic introduction to Jesus, his message of salvation, and Christianity in general. My own history with the Alpha process began many years ago, and my ongoing experience has cemented for me the power of this tool.

The first time I went through Alpha, it was so much fun. It had an incredible impact on me personally: it helped me fall deeper in love with Jesus, drew me to the Scriptures, improved my prayer life, and helped me gain a deeper understanding of the Holy Spirit. My first Alpha experience was in a home at the invitation of a generous couple, Bruce and Marilyn Havell, who were nondenominational evangelical Christians and so I didn't see how it would help me to *help others* fall more deeply in love with the Catholic faith—and that was my calling and passion. I wasn't innovative enough to see how to integrate Alpha into my mission as a Catholic.

Around that time, I ran into Fr. James Mallon, an old friend, and we ended up talking about how we could help people come to know Jesus. Bringing them to Mass didn't seem to be effective because, as Fr. James pointed out, the Mass was only intended for those fully initiated into the Church—for Catholics themselves. It's not meant for—and is often not meaningful for—people who don't have faith. That left me wondering, though, what I was supposed to do in order to bring people to Christ.

Fr. James said that the work of the rest of the week was to reach out and share Jesus with others. I asked him what he was doing throughout the week to bring others to Christ and how he was equipping the people in his parish to do the same. Like many of us, he wasn't doing anything in particular.

At that moment, a light switched on for me. I knew that I had something he could use, so I told him he should try running Alpha. He said he'd look into it, but I pushed and said he *had* to try it. He had the unique opportunity to do what I had been unable to do: anchor the Alpha program in the Church so that people whose lives were transformed through Alpha had a place to go and a place to grow.

After that conversation, Fr. James started running Alpha in his parish. Around the same time, I moved to New Brunswick, where I was reintroduced to Alpha through the Wesleyan Church. Pastor Tim Guptil invited me to a planning meeting for a regional Alpha conference to be held in the Maritime provinces in Canada. He and his team were looking for a Catholic networking coordinator to connect with the dioceses and parishes in the area, encouraging them to come to the conference. I saw myself as an unconnected nobody, so I said no. I told them they should reach out to the diocesan offices—they were well connected and could mobilize people.

Pastor Tim looked me in the eye and said, "Ron, we did, and they don't want anything to do with us." It broke my heart. I enjoyed building bridges between Catholics and non-Catholics. I agreed to come to one meeting, hear their plan, and then help them find the right person for the job.

When I showed up for the meeting, I was given a folder with my name on it, and in that folder was a booklet called *Alpha in a Catholic Context.* The booklet was created by David Nodar, who had originally brought Alpha to North America. I couldn't believe it. No one else had it in their folder. I took it out and devoured it; everything it said made sense. The booklet inspired me, but even more, it made me determined to fill that upcoming conference with nothing but Catholics!

Needless to say, that didn't happen, but I did manage to bring a delegation of ten people from my local Catholic church. The emcee asked people to stand up, denomination by denomination, and as they did, everyone cheered for them. When they asked the Catholics to stand up, we did, although I felt we had failed because of our small numbers. I felt terrible, but to my surprise, the applause for our delegation was much louder and longer than for all the other groups. I leaned over to someone who wasn't Catholic and asked what was going on. He said that they'd been praying for Catholics to join them for years and years, and we were the first who had.

Within a few years, not only were Catholics coming to that conference, but we actually hosted it and filled half the seats! The simple request to bring Catholics to that conference sparked something with deep roots. Eventually I saw how Alpha could work in a Catholic context. My heart burned for a way that I might help others within the Catholic Church encounter Jesus as I had—and Alpha provided that way.

A few years later, I ran into Fr. James again, and we discovered that we were both using Alpha as a tool to grow our communities. Fr. James told me that his priestly ministry was transformed through Alpha—it gave him a tool to bring people to Christ in a way he'd never seen before. He also informed me that he wished he could hire me as his director of evangelization so that he could wind me up and set me loose. We both laughed it off because we knew from experience that Catholics were leery of the word "evangelization"—and Fr. James didn't have the money in his budget anyway.

Ten years later, I was working in the pharmaceutical industry when I got a call from Fr. James. He was at a conference where Nicky Gumbel, the Anglican priest who had developed Alpha into its current format, was speaking. Fr. James had been hit by the Holy Spirit and was so inspired that, in the middle of the talk, he had gotten up from his front row seat and stepped out to call me. He'd just been assigned to Saint Benedict, a new parish in Halifax, and he asked if I would join him in ministry as the director of evangelization.

I sat in shocked silence long enough for Fr. James to think that the call had dropped. I knew that my financial responsibilities at the time wouldn't allow me to take on this role full-time, but I wanted a day or two to discern how I could make it work. Fr. James said that whether it was part-time, full-time, or whatever arrangement we could manage, he was convinced we needed to work together.

I called Fr. James back the next day. I said that if he was asking me to come and help him grow *a* church, I wasn't interested. But if he felt God was calling us together to work to impact *the* Church, I was all in. We were on exactly the same wavelength about the mission God was calling us to in that moment. This began our journey together at Saint Benedict.

The first item on our agenda was launching Alpha. We did it, and the life of the parish began to change from that very day. Alpha was the catalyst for this change.

From time to time when Fr. James and I would run into each other at work, we'd take a moment to share how excited we were to be part of a parish like this. This was the kind of Church we'd always wanted to belong to. We knew it was way bigger than anything he or I could ever do; it was the work of God through the power of the Holy Spirit.

Alpha is a small but important piece of a bigger puzzle for Catholics and, done well, it unleashes faith that is contagious, filled with joy, and incredibly fruitful. Our Divine Renovation Network parishes are not "Alpha parishes"; they are healthy evangelizing parishes. Therefore we prioritize evangelization and leadership development. **Alpha just happens to be the tool we use because we've found that nothing works better at both**

evangelizing and raising up leaders who can change our culture and take people from lukewarm to "on fire."

If we evangelize and develop leaders well, we will impact the rest of our parish culture—in everything from outreach and social justice to developing new and life-giving ministries to fostering an ever-deepening love for the sacraments. If you want to see your parish culture transformed; to evangelize those in the parish, those away from the Church, and those who don't know Jesus; and if you want to create a pipeline to form leaders to serve in your parish and build others up, I strongly recommend Alpha.

Maybe you've never heard of Alpha and are curious. Maybe you've experienced Alpha and want to know how best to use it within the life of your parish. Fr. James and I decided to write this book because we are convinced that Alpha, done well, can be an essential component of cultural change and transformation. We hope that what you find in the following pages will inspire you, and take some of the guesswork out of how to use Alpha as a powerful tool to enrich the soil of your parish.

Chapter One

Setting the Stage

FR. JAMES MALLON

As a priest engaged in parish ministry for nearly two decades, I have longed to see the Holy Spirit at work in the lives of parishioners. Like any pastor or anyone involved in pastoral ministry, I have also wanted to see the good news of the gospel draw the lost and the searching into the life of the Christian community. Two questions have influenced my thinking: Can Catholic parishes become communities of missionary disciples that bear lasting fruit? If so, what does it take to move them in that direction?

In my book *Divine Renovation: Bringing Your Parish from Maintenance to Mission*, I answered the first of these questions with a resounding *yes*—Catholic parishes can indeed become missionary and fruit-bearing. I answered the second question—how to accomplish this—by describing the renewal in my own parish, Saint Benedict in Halifax, Nova Scotia. I mention that book here because Alpha played a role in Saint Benedict's transformation, and I believe it can help other Catholic parishes too. *Unlocking Your Parish: Making Disciples, Raising Up Leaders with Alpha* aims to provide insight into what Alpha can offer the Catholic parish interested in becoming a mission-focused community.

Globally, over the past several years, we have seen parishes rediscover the call to "go . . . and make disciples" (Matthew 28:19), but as a universal Church, we have barely begun to respond to the Lord's call of renewal. If it were simply a matter of tweaking our processes and changing our activities as we continue to live out our current models of parish life, we might be further along. But our present situation requires far more than minor course corrections and better programming. It calls for a fundamental change of culture—a change in how we understand the world around us and how we understand what it means to be Catholic.

Living in a Change of Age

Throughout the course of history, there have been watershed moments that have shifted the direction of civilizations and profoundly affected our physical, intellectual, and spiritual lives. These moments—such as the inventions of the printing press and the steam engine—have often displaced or greatly altered the self-understanding and cultural underpinnings of what came before. Currently we are at another watershed moment that is radically altering secular culture and the assumptions people make about themselves, the world they live in, and the meaning of life.

Recognizing this profound shift, observers have said we are no longer living in an age of change; rather we are living through the change of an age. This new age has a number of names. Some call it the age of secularism; others use the term post-Christian or postmodern. Whatever its name, the reality is that this age is very different from what has come before.

Throughout much of its history, the Church in the West has existed in the cultural soil of Christendom, where the dominant cultural forces supported Christianity and even gave it a privileged place. There was, in the culture of Christendom, a sense of the transcendent importance of hierarchy, an appreciation for the natural law, and a deeply held belief in the universality of truth.

Our current culture, however, embraces a kind of scientific materialism that claims that all truth is relative. In other words, there is nothing objective about truth; it is entirely subjective. What is true for me is true for me, and what is true for you is true for you—even if our truths are mutually exclusive. This has obvious implications for the Church, which claims that there is, in fact, objective truth that serves the good of all peoples.

And so the question becomes: how should the Church respond to this new age and its very secular outlook?

Vatican II: The Church's Prophetic Response

This isn't the place for a historical retrospective, but briefly, we can see that the seeds of the cultural shift we are living through can be found early in the twentieth century. World War I cast a shadow over Europe; the resulting geopolitical instability set the stage for World War II and the horror of the Holocaust. Other wars and genocides followed, shattering the myth of the progressive improvement of human nature. Cultural forces converged around this time to accelerate social change on a massive scale: the sexual revolution, a growing drug culture, the reach of television into every home—all of these things created a kind of perfect storm that sent shock waves through Western culture.

In the midst of all this, the Holy Spirit inspired Pope John XXIII to call an ecumenical council of the Church. The documents that came out of the council's discussions contained the building blocks for a renewed engagement with the world and a framework for sharing the gospel message with contemporary societies. Fifty years later, we are finally beginning to understand more broadly and implement locally the Vatican Council's call to holiness and mission.

And therein lies the crux of our current situation. As dioceses and parishes, we continue to live and act as if we are still planted within the soil of Christendom. In the past, within the supporting cultural framework of Christendom, parishes could be communities of maintenance, where people passively received the sacraments and some religious formation. As I wrote in *Divine Renovation*,

> Culture supported faith and church attendance. . . . We just had to build it and people would come. . . . As long as we would go and open churches, there were always new communities of migrants and new babies. As long as we baptized and taught in our schools, we pumped out good "practicing Catholics." In a sense, we got away with not making disciples, because the culture propped it all up.[1]

This is why Catholic parish life in the fifties, sixties, and even to a certain extent in the seventies seems so vibrant to us in retrospect. The culture supported religious practice. Furthermore, in North America, Catholicism was still very much a religion of immigrants. Living away from their families and the traditions of the various countries from which they came to North America, these immigrant Catholics clung together. The parish became the center of social life, and participation in Catholic life helped reinforce a sense of belonging and familiar cultural and ethnic traditions.

In addition to reaffirming and deepening cultural and social bonds among Catholic immigrant groups, one of the goals of the Church was to help Catholics integrate into the larger North American societies where they lived. Churches built structures, like schools, to accomplish this kind of mainstreaming. The problem was that the larger culture was changing radically. With the unravelling and end of Christendom, the pastoral tools and approaches that we had previously employed became ineffective. Unfortunately, we haven't replaced them with much that seems to bear fruit.

The numbers bear this out. The Pew Research Center undertook a sociological study in 2015 and determined that 50 percent of millennials who were raised Catholic have jettisoned any connection to the Catholic faith, and for every person who enters the Catholic Church at Easter, six leave.[2] But we don't need statistics to see this reality—the faithful in North America are living it. Fewer and fewer Catholics are attending Mass, and sadly, the Sacrament of Confirmation has become ritualized apostasy, with most young people leaving any practice of their faith right after receiving the sacrament. In addition, most dioceses are in a process of retrenchment—combining multiple parishes into new administrative structures or placing the responsibilities of multiple parishes on the backs of lone priests.

This is a true moment of crisis but one of tremendous opportunity as well. If our primary reaction is to respond administratively and create new structures to slow our decline, then we might as well hang it all up now. We can't keep doing what we have always been doing and just doing it in more efficient ways. But if we see in this crisis an opportunity to let go of our previous pastoral models and embrace new approaches that place our structures and processes at the service of evangelization and mission, we will see new life.

Pope Francis seems to be calling the Church to this vision. In his apostolic exhortation *Evangelii Gaudium* (The Joy of the Gospel), he writes,

> I dream of a "missionary option," that is, a missionary impulse capable of transforming everything, so that the Church's customs, ways of doing things, times and schedules, language and structures can be suitably channeled for the evangelization of today's world rather than for her self-preservation.[3]

A Kind of Dying

Embracing this kind of change may mean letting go of many of the cultural hallmarks that have characterized Catholic parish life over the past decades. It may mean taking a hard look at our image of the priesthood and of pastoral ministry and also reexamining our fundamental assumptions about the ministerial work that we do. This is not easy stuff; it is a kind of dying. Walking this path toward a missionary culture is a clear embrace of the paschal mystery.

It is an essential surrender. Paul talks about this paradox of ministry in his Second Letter to the Corinthians: "For we who live are constantly being given up to death for the sake of Jesus, so that the life of Jesus may be manifested in our mortal flesh" (4:11).

We must intentionally enter into this lifestyle of surrender, not only personally, but communally. We must be willing to sacrifice to the Lord even that which may seem integral to our parish life—our buildings, processes, ministries, and ways of doing things. Our goal is not simply efficiency or keeping our parishes viable but rather freeing us to respond to the needs of men and women today. In this way, the life-changing power of the gospel can be unleashed through us.

Jesus told us we would experience the knife: "I am the true vine, and my Father is the vine grower. He takes away every branch in me that does not bear fruit, and every one that does he prunes so that it bears more fruit" (John 15:1-2). When we become connected more to our model than to our mission, we need this pruning so that more of his life can be manifested through us.

The Church's missionary impulse lies within the very nature of God, who is love. Love always pours itself out for others. This is why the Word of God left the glory of heaven and pitched his tent among us, choosing to live through our human nature, to suffer, die, and rise from the dead. He did it all so that we might be freed from the power of sin and be filled with God's own life.

Essentially, we are a missionary people because we belong to a missionary God. The question becomes: How can we, who have received the very life of Jesus, authentically manifest that missionary identity?

The Frozen Chosen

Part of our challenge in answering that question is the reality that many Catholics, including some within our leadership, have not encountered the love of the Father in Jesus Christ. They do not see themselves as beloved sons and daughters of God, and they may not have made an intentional choice to follow Jesus. In fact, many Catholics today see faith not in terms of their relationship with God and others but primarily as something that places moral demands on them. They adopt an almost servile mentality, focusing on the things they must do for God rather than responding in gratitude for the things that God has done in and for and through them.

This can make it difficult for parishes to live out their mission, since the overwhelming focus becomes how do *I* get to heaven. Many of our people don't see themselves as being part of a larger story—the story of salvation. They don't see themselves as being part of a Church that Jesus sent out on a mission, a Church that the Lord empowered by pouring out his Spirit. The idea that baptized Catholics are loved and are able to be channels of God's supernatural healing, mercy, forgiveness, providence, and justice or that they have an essential and unique role to play in the Church's mission—these are foreign concepts to many Catholics.

This truly is an issue of identity. Jesus explicitly rebuked the image of slavery in relationship to God when he told his disciples, "I no longer call you slaves, because a slave does not know what his master is doing. I have called you friends, because I have told you everything I have heard from my Father" (John 15:15). There is a new intimacy with the Father that comes with life in Jesus Christ and the promise of his Spirit. That is why, when his disciples asked Jesus to teach them how to pray, he gave them the words of the Our Father.

The apostle Paul affirms this reality in his letter to the Church in Rome:

> For those who are led by the Spirit of God are children of God.
> For you did not receive a spirit of slavery to fall back into fear,
> but you received a spirit of adoption, through which we cry,
> "Abba, Father!" The Spirit itself bears witness with our spirit
> that we are children of God, and if children, then heirs, heirs
> of God and joint heirs with Christ, if only we suffer with him
> so that we may also be glorified with him. (Romans 8:14-17)

Part of the work of evangelization and mission, then, is to help our people experience and embrace who they are as sons and daughters of God. The depths of their identity can be unlocked only in an encounter with Jesus Christ. Fostering such an encounter and supporting their journey toward Christ will, in turn, propel them out on mission.

The Right Tool for the Job

When Ron Huntley told me about Alpha, I was curious. But when I found out that it was not a Catholic initiative, I was hesitant and skeptical. When I played the VHS tape (remember those days?) and heard all the English accents, I immediately had to deal with another natural bias: the fact that I had been born and raised in Scotland. Through God's grace I was able to move past these biases within my own heart as I heard the gospel articulated in a simple and compelling way. The proof, however, was in the pudding.

From the very first time I ran Alpha in a parish, even though we made lots of mistakes, we saw God work through it in a powerful way. We saw transformed lives and soon began to feel that our parish was being transformed. Here, clearly, was an effective response to the challenging times in which we live. The current situation within the Church, the state of secular culture around us, and the urgent call to mission that we have received from Christ demand a response. The Second Vatican Council and our last four popes have reiterated that call to mission. We have found Alpha to be one of the most powerful and effective tools for responding to it, both in reaching those who are far from the Church and in helping Catholics discover their identity in Christ. Moreover, Alpha can be a tremendous catalyst for changing the culture of a parish and helping transform the fundamental model of ministry.

But a word of caution: if Alpha is just one parish program among many that the pastor is encouraging people to attend, it will not bear as much fruit as it could. Alpha's potential to change culture is unlocked when the parish uses it as the foundation for a larger strategy. That strategy should focus on adult evangelization and connect with other activities that foster discipleship and mission.

I often find myself saying this when I speak to priests and pastoral leaders: evangelization is the pump that drives everything, and Alpha is a powerful evangelizing process. You can't ever let go of that pump if you truly want to foster renewal and transformation. If you evangelize, it will change your parish's weekend experience—not only how people participate in the Mass but also how parishioners handle everything from hospitality to managing the parking lot. If you evangelize, you will build up your Alpha team and raise up leaders. If you evangelize, people will become hungry for community and service. It has been my experience that people who come through the Alpha process clamor for community!

The time has come for us to stop using pastoral models that try to feed people who don't even know they're hungry. Instead we need to use evangelizing methods that allow God to stir up the hunger for him that already exists within every human soul. In the following chapters, we'll share with you some of the ways we have used Alpha to make disciples, raise up leaders, and foster renewal in the parishes where we work.

Chapter Two

Mission, Evangelization, and Alpha

FR. JAMES MALLON

Stephen Covey, author of *The 7 Habits of Highly Effective People*, once said that "the main thing is to keep the main thing the main thing."[4] That's something we've tried to do both at Saint Benedict Parish and in our work through the Divine Renovation Ministry. But what is the main thing? That's the question we need to ask ourselves constantly, at all levels of the Church today.

Why? Because at the parish and diocesan level, there are so many things going on—multiple requests for our time and attention, administrative tasks that need completing, programs and processes to run, and so on. Our busyness makes it easy for us to lose track of the essential focus of the Church.

What is that focus? Jesus made it abundantly clear when he commissioned his disciples before ascending to the Father:

All power in heaven and on earth has been given to me. Go, therefore, and make disciples of all nations, baptizing them in the name of the Father, and of the Son, and of the holy Spirit, teaching them to observe all that I have commanded you. And behold, I am with you always, until the end of the age. (Matthew 28:18-20)

The mission of the Church is to make disciples. Fr. Simon Lobo, a good friend and the current pastor of Saint Benedict Parish, defines a disciple as "someone who has had a life-changing experience of God and made the decision to surrender and follow him." At the heart of this decision is an encounter with Christ that leads one into a personal relationship with the Father in the power of the Holy Spirit.

Although many Catholics struggle with this personal language, it comes right out of our Tradition. Pope Benedict XVI, in his encyclical *Deus Caritas Est*, wrote: "Being Christian is not the result of an ethical choice or a lofty idea, but the encounter with an event, a person, which gives life a new horizon and a decisive direction."[5] He built on a foundation left by his predecessor, Pope John Paul II, who taught that "the new evangelization is not a matter of merely passing on doctrine but rather of a personal and profound meeting with the Savior."[6]

We see the personal dimensions of this relationship most clearly in the words of the Savior himself, when he instructed his disciples, "Whoever loves me will keep my word, and my Father will love him, and we will come to him and make our dwelling with him" (John 14:23). This intimate connection between God and us reaches its highest expression in the Eucharist, where we receive the Body and Blood, Soul and Divinity, of Jesus. You can't get more personal than that!

Mission Critical

It is in the context of this personal relationship with God that men and women experience love, mercy, healing, freedom, and transformation, gradually growing in their desire to be channels of that love for others. This work of making disciples, which the Church calls evangelization, draws people into the love of the Father in Jesus Christ and prepares them to recognize and receive this love. When they do, their response can reshape businesses, societies, and cultures in such a way that they foster all that is authentically human.

This work isn't about preserving our parishes or our structures or about relying on our history as we consider our future. The mission of the Church is about the salvation of people and the transformation of the world. We need to rediscover a sense of urgency about this. It's one thing to say the Church has a mission. While this statement acknowledges the importance of mission, it actually places the existence of the Church before the reality of that mission. In many of our parishes, for example, there might be an acknowledgment that we as Catholics are called to mission, but often our people seem to think that the mission either is directed primarily at the members of our parish community or is something we can figure out after we take care of the important work of maintaining the life of our community.

Pope Paul VI saw things differently. He understood the primacy of mission when he wrote, "Evangelizing is in fact the grace and vocation proper to the Church, her deepest identity. She exists in order to evangelize."[7] Evangelizing isn't just an activity of the Church; it is a component of her essence. Indeed, the

Church emerges out of the mission-saturated life of Christ. We see in the moment of the Church's birth at Pentecost a movement outward: the gospel message is shared in every tongue, and three thousand are added in a single day (see Acts 2:1-41)!

It is not so much that the Church has a mission but rather that the mission of Christ has a Church. Our common life together, our identity as a people called by God and united to him in baptism, cannot be fully realized unless we leave the comfort of our communities and share Jesus with the world. It is high time that the Church became more fully who she was created to be!

Fostering Encounter

In my travels across the world, I'm often asked how we can we get young people back to Mass. Clearly, we as Church are feeling the demographic pinch. In most parishes, the average age of members continues to increase, and fewer and fewer young families are participating in parish activities and sacramental celebrations.

I understand the concern behind the question; I know that it comes from an authentic place. However, it is rooted in a maintenance-focused mindset. How do we get (insert Group A) to participate in our practices? How can we get those people over there to come to us?

The truth is, we are asking the wrong questions. Rather than wondering what we can do to get people to come to church, we should be asking how we can help them enter into a relationship with Jesus. What can we do to foster and sustain an encounter with the risen Christ?

For too long Catholics have relied on the correctness of the Church's teaching to draw people in. "We have the truth," our people say, and we wonder why the world doesn't rush the doors of our parishes to receive it. That approach may have worked in a previous age, when there was a shared cultural appreciation for objective truth. However, postmodernists (especially millennials) don't care about *the* truth; they care about *their* truth. Any attempt at evangelizing postmodernists must, therefore, begin by meeting them where they are. The Church must make every effort to encounter people and walk with them, as Jesus did with the two disciples on the road to Emmaus (see Luke 24:13-35).

This is about building authentic relationships with men and women who may believe things quite antithetical to the Church's teaching. It is about investing in their lives first, not about requiring them to pass a Church orthodoxy test before we will reach out and include them. It's about making a space for them once they arrive and inviting them to experience something fundamentally human. This is the essence of hospitality, and hospitality lies at the heart of love.

It is only when we build these relationships, when we create a sense of belonging, that we earn the right to share what we believe with other people—and this sharing must not be merely a matter of dogma, doctrine, morality, or teaching. We must share Jesus himself, in our actions and in our words. We must testify to what Christ has done for the world and how that has manifested in our own lives. We must pass on the heart of the gospel message, which the Church calls the kerygma.

Pope John Paul II defined the kerygma as "the initial ardent proclamation by which a person is one day overwhelmed and brought to the decision to entrust himself to Jesus Christ by faith."[8] The kerygma, then, is a proclamation of good news that awakens faith, opens the heart to God, and leads one to make a decision to follow Jesus. When this happens, transformation occurs.

Many Catholics struggle with this belong-believe-behave model of evangelization. They expect people to *behave* and *believe* a particular way before they can *belong*. Furthermore, our people are reticent about sharing their belief in God with others; for them faith is both personal and private—not to be shared but to be relegated to the same status as sex and politics when it comes to "polite" conversation. Those Catholics who might be interested in sharing Jesus with others feel ill-equipped and therefore don't make the attempt. Or if they do, they treat different beliefs as invaders that must be repelled; they often lead with arguments and apologetics.

Here is where Alpha can change the game in your parish. The genius of the Alpha process is that it fosters trust and authentic relationships within its small groups while it gradually proclaims the kerygma and reveals the heart of the Father in Jesus Christ. As I wrote in *Divine Renovation*,

> A look under the hood of Alpha reveals that the secret to its success is that it embraces the belong-believe-behave approach to evangelization. It is perfectly suited for the post-modern mindset. The first goal of Alpha is to create a warm, welcoming, non-threatening, non-pressurized and nonjudgmental environment where guests are loved and accepted unconditionally. They are given permission, by word and example, to be authentic and real. No one will correct them for their unorthodox (or even

crazy) beliefs, their doubts or their struggles. There will be no judgment about their lifestyles.

Through the ten-week process, trust begins to build as meals are shared and participants experience being listened to in small groups. As the sense of belonging grows, they begin to let down their guard and receive the message of the talks. At this point, the truth of Jesus and his Gospel begins to knock on the door of their hearts, and by the end of the ten weeks, the process has led many of them to a personal encounter with Jesus and to a decision to follow him. What happens after this transformation of belief is a total re-evaluation of lifestyle and behavior, as the journey of discipleship begins.[9]

Furthermore, when you place Alpha at the heart of your evangelization strategy and use it to raise up leaders in your parish, you will find that it helps your parishioners learn how to accompany others on a journey of faith. Through Alpha, they will learn how to meet people where they are, listen wholeheartedly, share the essential core of the gospel message, and pray with others. In many ways, using Alpha demystifies the process of evangelization and makes it accessible to ordinary Catholics.

Often parishioners who become Alpha leaders are shocked to discover that they have become missionary disciples. Perhaps they expected missionary discipleship to be an arcane and exceedingly rare state that only the super holy could reach. In fact, it is the grounding vocation of all the baptized!

But It's Not Catholic!

Alpha is not a silver bullet; it's a tool. When used as part of a larger pastoral strategy, it is the best tool that I have found for jump-starting and sustaining parish renewal. Despite this, I occasionally experience significant resistance to using Alpha from pastors, priests, and pastoral leaders. This resistance can be summed up in the following phrase: *but it's not Catholic!*

While this is true on a literal level—the Alpha course emerged out of Holy Trinity Brompton, an Anglican parish in London—the protest isn't primarily about the fact that we didn't think of it. Rather the critique behind the "it's not Catholic" objection rests on the notion that Alpha, as an Anglican-invented process, does not reflect the richness, fullness, and integrity of the Catholic Church's theology and teaching.

This critique of Alpha bears further discussion. I believe that Catholics evaluate Alpha incorrectly on four levels.

To Evangelize or to Catechize?

The first and perhaps biggest issue has to do with our expectations of Alpha. Multiple generations of North American Catholics have focused primarily on catechesis, particularly in regard to the implementation of the Second Vatican Council's liturgical norms. Furthermore, as I have said, our parishes and dioceses have adopted a culture of maintenance in response to the sweeping secularization of our larger society. Within that maintenance culture, we have prioritized orthodoxy and the correct transmission of Church teaching. We see solid catechesis as the primary way in which the Church will survive and grow in our current age. Therefore we want our programs to be catechetically rich and comprehensive, reflecting the fullness of our theology.

Of course, there is nothing wrong with the desire for solid catechesis! When we evaluate Alpha primarily through the lens of that desire, however, we will be disappointed, because Alpha won't deliver the things that we expect it to. That's not accidental; it's by design. The reality is that Alpha is not a catechetical tool but rather a tool of evangelization rooted in kerygmatic proclamation.

In the early Church, there was a distinction between the proclamation (kerygma) of the apostles and their teaching (Didache). As I mentioned earlier in this chapter, it is the kerygmatic proclamation that awakens faith. Catechesis—the intellectual, spiritual, human, and pastoral formation in the life of a disciple—then roots an individual in Christ's body, the Church.

John Paul II put it this way: "The definitive aim of catechesis is to put people not only in touch but in communion, in intimacy, with Jesus Christ."[10] But healthy relationships have a kind of rhythm. Before one can become truly intimate with another person, one has to be introduced to that person.

The Church has always recognized this essential rhythm and the place of evangelization in the introductory role. The *General Directory for Catechesis* highlights the evangelization process:

> The Church, while ever containing in herself the fullness of the means of salvation, always operates "by slow stages." The conciliar decree *Ad Gentes* clarifies well the dynamic of the process of evangelization: Christian witness, dialogue and presence in charity (11-12), the proclamation of the Gospel and the call

to conversion (13), the catechumenate and Christian Initiation (14), the formation of the Christian communities through and by means of the sacraments and their ministers (15–18). This is the dynamic for establishing and building up the Church.[11]

Alpha's framework creates a process that combines witness, dialogue, and presence with the proclamation of the gospel. It is not primarily concerned with the catechumenate, with Christian initiation, or with theological formation, but rather with the initial introduction of individuals to the person of Jesus Christ. In his apostolic exhortation *Evangelii Gaudium*, Pope Francis reminds us of the foundational nature of this kerygmatic proclamation:

> This first proclamation is called "first" not because it exists at the beginning and can then be forgotten or replaced by other more important things. It is first in a qualitative sense because it is the principal proclamation.[12]

The kerygma is the essential, or core, message of Jesus Christ. It is not a summary of the *Catechism*. Some Catholics who look at the topics for Alpha talks criticize it for that reason. But if we held ourselves to the same standard, neither the Apostles Creed nor the Nicene Creed would pass muster.

Others say that the Alpha videos teach incorrectly about the nature of the Church, salvation, and the sacraments. However, a close examination of the content of Alpha reveals that it isn't what is said that Catholics find problematic but what is *not* said. Again, Alpha is a kerygmatic process and is not designed to capture the fullness of Church teaching. *Not saying something is not the same as saying something erroneous.* It isn't a deficiency but rather part of a pedagogical methodology.

When proclaiming the good news to someone who has never heard or responded to it, for example, it is enough to say that Christ died for our sins. We don't have to dive into a comparative critique of penal substitutionary atonement versus the satisfaction theory of atonement as articulated by St. Anselm. The reality of Christ's love for the individual is communicated by that simple proclamation. Further study on God's methodology for our salvation may deepen the love that a disciple has for God but may overwhelm someone who is just beginning a journey toward the Lord.

The Basics

A second but related issue that some Catholics have with Alpha is that, for well-formed Catholics, it seems "too basic," and therefore not valuable. I think it is important to remember that Alpha is not a tool designed primarily for those within the Church. It is not a program of adult faith formation, education, or enrichment. Alpha was created to help the unchurched and those far away from a formal religious experience (which is a rapidly growing segment of our population) build authentic relationships with Christians and have an encounter with Jesus that leads to conversion. When a parish engages in any pastoral activity it needs to ask itself if it is trying to catch fish (evangelization) or feed sheep (discipleship), because fish don't eat grass and sheep don't eat worms!

Of course, Alpha can be fruitful for Catholics. I have seen thousands of Catholic men and women whose lives have been changed through their participation in Alpha. It is possible, however, to use a mission-focused tool with a maintenance mindset. When that happens, Catholics can miss the power of this tool. Because it is "not for them," they think it's not really for anybody!

Embracing the Process

Thirdly, Catholics who analyze Alpha primarily for theological content tear at the integrity of the Alpha *process,* which is at the core of Alpha's mission to help people encounter Christ. This process is built on the belong-believe-behave paradigm. In Alpha, the process is as important as the content. Belonging (the experience of hospitality and community in the context of a meal) leads to a gradual unveiling of the good news of Jesus Christ (believing). If participants are open, they grow in trust, and their belief is shaped by profound experiences of God.

The small group component of Alpha is also essential. It is low-key and conversational in style, making it a most appropriate tool for working with postmodernists (especially millennials). Alpha discussions are not the time for Catholic participants to correct non-Catholics in their beliefs or share Catholic teaching. When the process unfolds as intended, the encounter with Jesus leaves participants with a hunger for more community and a greater openness and even desire to hear what the Church teaches (behave).

Insider Perspective

Finally, well-formed Catholics who see the "incompleteness" of Alpha's approach to Church teaching may be seeing issues that are real from their perspective but that are not being experienced by unformed Catholics, non-Catholic Christians, and the unchurched. Our insider perspective can cloud our judgment regarding the effects and "side effects" of using something like Alpha.

I'll never forget the time I was doing a parish internship as a seminarian and attended a catechist evening of formation. The evening featured a video meant to help us understand and use the soon-to-be-released *Catechism of the Catholic Church*. As I watched the video through the lens of my advanced theological training, I began to see numerous ways in which it could blunt the clarity of the upcoming *Catechism*. I became quite upset— fuming might even be a better word. I couldn't wait to get into a small group with other participants and express my outrage. Imagine my surprise when I did just that and found out that no one had any idea what I was speaking about and, rather, that they found the video exceptionally helpful and were excited to have the *Catechism* shape their catechetical approach!

A Symphony of Truth

Beyond these four major critiques of Alpha, some Catholics resist using Alpha within the parish solely because it comes from a Protestant source. I think we must be very careful here. Is it possible that we have become so blind as to believe that God cannot work outside the Catholic Church? Are we like the Jews of Jesus' time who were obstinate and frustrated when Jesus pointed out to them the times the Lord showed his favor to the Gentiles? Of course, the difference between Catholic and non-Catholic Christians is nowhere as great as the difference between Jews and Gentiles. As *Lumen Gentium* taught, although the Church of Christ subsists in the Catholic Church, there is only one Church of Christ.[13]

As it turns out, truth is symphonic! What Alpha offers is an expression of that catholic (that is, universal) truth. In other words, there is no such thing as the Catholic kerygma or the Protestant kerygma. There is only the proclamation of one and the same gospel message, which belongs to the entire body of Christ. When proclaimed, it brings the whole body closer to the visible unity Jesus prayed for.

A Proposition

I understand the hesitancy to take on Alpha because it comes from a Protestant source. As I mentioned, when I first encountered Alpha, I had to overcome that bias too. I'm a Catholic from Scotland! This whole thing came from Anglicans, and there was this English guy featured in all the videos!

But when I began to run Alpha in my parishes and witnessed its power to bring others to an encounter with Jesus Christ, I saw what an amazing tool it really is for our current situation. In my experience, there is no greater process for reaching the unchurched and our own communities of faith with the life-changing power of the gospel.

Chapter Three

Alpha and Parish Transformation

RON HUNTLEY

"Have you accepted Jesus Christ as your personal Lord and Savior?"

No other question seems to trigger a fight-or-flight response from Catholics quite the way that one does! Many Catholics consider their faith both personal *and* private. Perhaps this is because, for many years, Catholics in North America worked hard at assimilating into the secular culture around us. Or perhaps we have become used to the idea that priests, deacons, and religious are supposed to do that sort of work (talking about Jesus), while we laypeople support their work financially and try to raise our families in the faith. Whatever the reasons, we have inherited a Catholic culture that places a value on *not* talking about God or our relationship with him. In fact, a sociological study done in the United States found that atheists talked about God more than Catholics did.[14]

In this kind of environment, openly talking about Jesus and asking others about their relationship with him seems foreign and intrusive. Catholics perceive the have-you-accepted-Jesus approach to speaking of faith as a kind of "gotcha" affair that puts people on the spot and applies an uncomfortable kind of pressure to get them to convert. Many of our people, seeing this sort of evangelistic effort on the part of other Christians, conclude that the Catholic Church shouldn't do evangelization. Or if they do understand that making disciples is indeed the mission of the Church, they believe that the Catholic approach must, by definition, be completely opposite—the silent approach. Look at the popularity of the oft-quoted advice from St. Francis to "preach the gospel at all times; when necessary use words." Never mind that St. Francis did not actually say this; many Catholics embrace it literally and rarely speak of their faith.

Given this kind of focus on the private nature of faith, our parish communities are often very inwardly oriented. We spend lots of time concentrating on maintaining the hallmarks of parish life. Outreach and evangelization, if done at all, are almost a secondary concern. Faith formation, if it is offered, consists largely of academically grounded programs primarily concerned with the intellectual understanding of Church teaching or Scripture.

Further, many Catholics are mostly familiar with formal prayers, such as those used in the Mass, and in devotions such as the Rosary; and as a result, they are uncomfortable leading others in prayer or saying a quick prayer with someone in need. They experience the Mass itself in a personal and individualized way, and often they don't participate much. When the celebration of the Mass is over, the community scatters, and the members continue living their separate lives. It's quite possible, for example, to be missing from the Sunday celebration for several weeks or longer and not have anyone notice or reach out. Bottom line: those who are interested in sharing their faith in Jesus with others feel ill-equipped to do so.

Drawing Others In

Change is hard, but it is needed in order to fulfill the call to become fruitful missionary communities. We can start by taking a look at the Church's understanding of evangelization and mission, which is far richer than we imagine. The bishops in the United States put it this way: evangelization "means bringing the Good News of Jesus into every human situation and seeking to convert individuals and society by the divine power of the Gospel itself."[15]

That may sound like a daunting definition, but it's really quite simple. I remember a conversation I had not long ago with the gentleman sitting next to me at a dinner. When I found out that he was Catholic, I asked if he had any exciting things going on at his parish. He gave me a list of activities, but as I listened, I couldn't hear anything that sounded like evangelization. When I asked him what they were doing to evangelize people, he said they were starting a couple of small groups.

That's not actually evangelization, I replied. He was clearly confused by my response and asked me what it means to evangelize. I said that evangelization is when you bring someone who is outside of a relationship with Jesus into a relationship with Jesus. He liked my definition but acknowledged that his church wasn't doing that because they were in a period of transition. He thought maybe they could try that in a couple of years. It broke my heart.

In the second chapter of Mark's Gospel, we hear the story of a paralyzed man who met Jesus, thanks to four resourceful friends. Up until that point, there wasn't a single thing these men could have done to help their paralyzed friend, but then they heard about this rabbi named Jesus who was healing people. So they got together, put their friend on a mat, and carried him into town.

They soon realized they had a problem—they couldn't get close to Jesus. By that point, Jesus was a bit of a rock star, and there was a crowd around him. The friends didn't let that obstacle get in their way. They climbed up on the roof of the house where Jesus was, cut a hole in the roof, and lowered the paralyzed man down to him. Can you imagine the faces of everyone in the crowd as this was happening? Jesus healed that man. He changed everything for him.

I don't know about you, but I want to be part of a Church where people love their friends so much and believe in Jesus so much that they'll do whatever it takes to bring those two together. That kind of persevering self-giving love can take root in and change the culture of your parish when you use Alpha intentionally as a tool for evangelization.

In many ways, Alpha mirrors Jesus' approach to ministry—especially in meeting people where they are, regardless of their social status or level of sanctity. In Luke 18:9-14, Jesus tells a story to a group of people who think pretty highly of themselves:

He then addressed this parable to those who were convinced of their own righteousness and despised everyone else. "Two people went up to the temple area to pray; one was a Pharisee and the other was a tax collector. The Pharisee took up his position and spoke this prayer to himself, 'O God, I thank you that I am not like the rest of humanity—greedy, dishonest, adulterous—or even like this tax collector. I fast twice a week, and I pay tithes on my whole income.' But the tax collector stood off at a distance and would not even raise his eyes to heaven but beat his breast and prayed, 'O God, be merciful to me a sinner.' I tell you, the latter went home justified, not the former; for everyone who exalts himself will be humbled, and the one who humbles himself will be exalted."

Unfortunately, when people finally work up the courage to go to church, they sometimes encounter the self-righteous types of people that Jesus was addressing. As a result, these unchurched people feel as if they don't belong and are being judged. Alpha can break through walls, helping parishioners develop a welcoming spirit and helping the unchurched and the searching put aside their fears.

During Alpha I eat dinner with the same people once a week, ten weeks in a row, and I see people getting to know each other for who they truly are. Everyone has time to drop the pretenses and suspicions and get comfortable with each other. Alpha makes it very simple.

For one thing, Alpha doesn't use lots of Church language. We don't hide behind religious jargon or words, and this helps our guests be vulnerable and free to share deeply personal stories from their lives. Their openness and honesty changes all of us and can help unite us. And so in Alpha, we teach our people to listen to others and learn to love them, whatever their background or level of religious interest. After all, what we're trying to do is make our parishes places where outsiders can feel respected and welcomed—not judged.

Alpha challenges us to expand the circle of people we care about. Jesus certainly challenged his disciples in this manner. We read about this in Matthew 12:46-50:

> While he was still speaking to the crowds, his mother and his brothers appeared outside, wishing to speak with him. [Someone told him, "Your mother and your brothers are standing outside, asking to speak with you."] But he said in reply to the one who told him, "Who is my mother? Who are my brothers?" And stretching out his hand toward his disciples, he said, "Here are my mother and my brothers. For whoever does the will of my heavenly Father is my brother, and sister, and mother."

Too many Catholics, busy with other priorities, give God as little time as possible—just enough to let them squeak into heaven and get their kids there too. Catholics often seem to be looking for the minimum requirements for salvation. This isn't necessarily their fault. It's probably related more to the fact that the Church doesn't seem to make a difference for many Catholics, let alone for people who don't know Jesus.

This Gospel story points to something different. It says that as you fall in love with Jesus, your circle of care expands. Church is not an organization you join but rather a family that you belong to. As you grow in love for Jesus, you will grow in love for others. As you sit at a table for ten weeks and have dinner with people, you do get to know them. In fact, you'll actually fall in love with them and see them as your brothers and sisters.

The whole idea of Alpha is to help people fall in love with Christ and be filled with the power of the Holy Spirit. When that begins to happen, the culture of your church starts to change.

Five Practical Ways Alpha Changes the Culture

Let's take a look at some of the practical changes that occur in parishes that use Alpha as part of a larger evangelization strategy.

1. Hospitality: A terrible thing happened to me the other day—I lost my job. One of my favorite jobs is being out in front of the church, opening the door and welcoming people as they arrive for Mass, even in a big Canadian storm. The other day, as I was rounding the corner to our door, I discovered Walter standing in my spot. Walter recently took Alpha and is now on our Alpha team. He's a big guy with a fantastic Fu Manchu moustache and a smile that could warm the coldest heart. There he was, greeting people, with the biggest smile on his face. After Mass he came up to me, practically giddy, to let me know how much he loved welcoming people at the door. It was so cool to see his enthusiasm. He's going to be received fully into the Church soon, but he is already excited about extending hospitality to those walking into our church.

As you train your Alpha teams and bring people through the Alpha process, they learn to be aware of the needs of guests and of the importance of offering radical hospitality to everyone. That's how Alpha transforms parish hospitality—something Walter experienced first as a guest on the receiving end and then as a team member on the giving end. Before and after Mass, and at every parish event, our Alpha teams actively look for guests who seem unsure or as if they might be feeling awkward. Then team members go over to welcome them and put them at ease.

2. Participation at Mass: Have you ever noticed that there is a difference between a dentist's office and a football game? I'm not just talking about what happens there either. One of the main differences is that very few people want to be at the dentist's office. A dental waiting room has an energy and "feel" quite distinctive from that of a football game, a place where people actually want to be. Sometimes our celebrations of the Mass have the feel of a dental surgery!

Fr. James says that when he was first ordained, he'd look out over the congregation during Mass and feel as if he was at a zombie convention. There was no interaction. Alpha can make a difference even here, in part because the Alpha process is highly interactive and helps people be at ease engaging with others and participating in group activities. More important, though, is the fact that the goal of the process is an encounter with Jesus Christ. When Alpha participants experience that encounter, they open up and discover a hunger for community and a deeper desire for the Lord's presence. If they are Catholic or thinking of becoming Catholic, they take what they learned and experienced at Alpha regarding interacting with others, and they transfer that to their participation at Mass.

I'm not just talking about the externals of participation, such as saying the responses or singing hymns and songs of praise (though those efforts definitely and noticeably increase as well) or even of participation that is personally and privately rewarding for the person. Rather we have seen that the openness of Alpha "alumni" as they worship God changes the experience of Mass for everyone. This shouldn't surprise us. It's good Catholic theology. The *Catechism* makes it clear:

> The fruit of sacramental life is both personal and ecclesial. For every one of the faithful on the one hand, this fruit is life for God in Christ Jesus; for the Church, on the other, it is an increase in charity and in her mission of witness. (1134)

Sherry Weddell explains it this way:

> For every one of us, the fruit we bear has a profound impact on our personal maturation and holiness as disciples in Christ. But your fruit also increases the evangelical capacity of the whole Church: her love and ability to bear witness to God.

In other words, in terms of the Mass, the more we participate with our whole hearts, the more the Mass can change everyone present—and the whole Church. If you have ever been to a Mass where a majority of the people actively want to be there and participate, you know what I am talking about. Imagine that happening at your parish!

3. Sharing of Gifts: Parishes frequently struggle to find people willing to share their gifts in the multitude of parish ministries. Many parishes can't possibly take on anything else because they just don't have enough people willing to step forward to do the work. What we find as we continue to run Alpha is an increasing pool of people who want to volunteer for ministry. I'm sure this is music to your ears!

Through Alpha, we first make a very generous contribution to people's lives. We love them. As they realize how much they're being loved, they respond by loving back. It's what people do! And it goes a long way toward changing the culture.

It is not just the quantity of people sharing gifts that changes but also the "quality." The men and women who start to step forward are not just doing so out of a sense of obligation or volunteerism. They do it out of a growing relationship with God, which impels them to share their gifts generously and *joyfully*. This joyful openness allows the Spirit of God to work through these folks, changing those with whom they come in contact. As that continues, it's like a cluster of small flames that ignite everything and everyone around them.

4. Prayer: Every baptized Catholic is called to pray. Prayer isn't simply an obligation for us; it's the very lifeblood of our relationship with God. Relationships require communication, and prayer is the most fundamental communication—speaking to God and listening. When we pray, we enter into the mystery of God's life and love for us.

That sounds really pious, but I have to be honest: for the longest time, I only knew how to pray prayers that were written out. Growing up, I prayed the Our Father, the Hail Mary, and the Guardian Angel Prayer with my mom every night before I went to bed, and I prayed the responses when we went to Mass on Sunday. But it wasn't until I was older—when I wanted to draw closer to Jesus, with whom I had fallen in love—that I discovered a desire to pray. We often see the same dynamic unfold for people who go through Alpha, whether they are Catholic or have never set foot in a church before. Prayer becomes real and personal for them, an expression of their relationship with God.

Alpha also changes the way we approach prayer as a community, because during Alpha we teach our teams how to pray not just *for* people but *with* them. Then, during two Alpha sessions, we give them the opportunity to pray with guests who want to receive prayer. When people learn how to pray with others or they experience others praying for them, they start to actively pray with people as they see a need. It begins to feel normal.

The other day, my friend Josh, a medical doctor, texted me. A coworker came into his office struggling with a significant problem. Josh mustered up the courage and offered to pray with him. To his surprise, the person said yes, and so Josh reached out and prayed. He texted me right after because he was excited that he had actually offered to pray and that someone said yes! He wrote that he had never felt more alive in his faith than when he prayed with that person in the name of Jesus Christ.

5. Fellowship: Fellowship may seem like a foreign word to many Catholics, but it just means an experience of community. We live in a world that is more connected by technology than ever before, and yet we are living in the most disconnected ways. There is a hunger in the human soul for community and authentic relationships. Responding to that hunger is one of the things that Alpha does really well. Journeying with a small group for ten weeks, wrestling with some of the fundamental questions of human life, forges a real bond. Vulnerability leads to intimacy.

These intimate bonds of friendship and community don't stay at the Alpha sessions. They are expressed anywhere members of that small group meet—both within and outside the parish community. These relationships really start to change things in the parish culture.

I remember a man who didn't know anyone at our parish, even though he'd been going to Saint Benedict since it had opened. He told me that he'd been coming to church for years just to sit in his pew, pray, and then go home. Nobody knew or cared that he was there—and that worked fine for him. Now, after Alpha, all of a sudden he couldn't show up at the parish without hugging half a dozen people on the way in and another half a dozen people on the way out. He loved the change he was experiencing, even though it wasn't something he had known he needed.

This was an incredibly positive experience for a man who sometimes found it difficult to connect in social situations. Alpha changed his experience of church and expanded his social network. He felt seen and welcomed by his new friends at the parish. This sense of fellowship and belonging increases when you use Alpha; it shapes how people perceive the Church and their place in it.

A few Easters ago, some out-of-town friends I had worked with were in the city. One person was from out west, another from Ontario, and the other from Prince Edward Island. I knew that they didn't have any family with them, so I invited them to our family dinner for Easter. All three said yes.

It was so beautiful being around this big table with my family. Yes, it included people who didn't share my bloodline, but they truly were my family. They are my brothers and sisters.

We're hearing that this sort of welcoming and sharing is happening all over our parish. We don't tell people to do it or try to guilt them into doing it. Through Alpha, people spontaneously build relationships.

So now that you've seen some of the ways that Alpha can impact your parish community, all you need to do is reserve your meeting rooms, start streaming the Alpha videos, and everything will change, right?

Well, . . . not really.

We'll talk about that in the next chapter!

Chapter Four

Alpha and Pastoral Strategy

RON HUNTLEY

"If you don't know where you are going, any road will get you there."

That quote doesn't actually appear in *Alice in Wonderland*, but it sums up an exchange between Alice and the Cheshire cat—Alice doesn't know where she wants to go, but she asks the cat how to get there. It captures the essence of what it's like to live without clear direction or goals. Have you ever been part of an organization, group, or community that had no vision? If so, then you know how extremely painful that experience can be.

Companies, communities, and in particular, parishes that don't have a clear vision or sense of mission end up wandering from activity to activity. Because there is little focus, tenacity, or sense of direction, morale suffers, people burn out, and little gets accomplished. Vision, on the other hand, galvanizes; it creates passion. Passion, it turns out, energizes a group to do what it takes to realize the vision.

When a parish has a compelling vision and supports that vision with a game plan that is solid, things begin to happen.

A compelling vision that is rooted in the will of God and supported by a good pastoral strategy, saturated with prayer, is more likely to yield amazing fruit. Every parish needs this sort of vision, tailored to its circumstances. But Alpha does not lay out a specific vision for a community. By itself, it isn't a whole pastoral strategy. It is a tool—one that becomes very powerful when used as a smaller piece of a much bigger puzzle.

Not Just Another Program

Too often we neglect an overall strategy and vision as we search for a single tool—the perfect tool—that will answer all our needs. We roam from program to program, on the lookout for that perfect tool. When the program we are currently using disappoints (as it always will because no one tool does everything), we abandon it in favor of the next promising tool.

I've seen this happen with Alpha. A parish will observe the success that other parishes are experiencing with Alpha and decide to give it a try, but they run it as just another program in a sea of programs. Generally the early adopters, people who are quick to try new things, jump on board and attend Alpha.

Over time the majority of active parishioners will take Alpha and by the fourth season, everyone who was open to taking Alpha will have done so, and numbers will decline. At that point, leadership will grow tired. Seeing the lack of interest as a sign that Alpha has run its course, they'll start looking for the next program.

This happens not only because parish leaders fail to understand Alpha's fundamental goal of helping people encounter Christ but also because parishes don't link Alpha to other parts of parish life. At Saint Benedict, we use Alpha to create a culture of invitation and to raise up Catholic disciples who become passionate about Jesus and the mission he has given us. Alpha is an essential tool within our larger strategy, the means through which we invite people into a relationship with Jesus and then help them grow in faith—in other words, we make disciples and then we form disciples.

You might wonder why we don't use the Mass as our primary means of helping people encounter Christ. Earlier I mentioned that people who aren't in a relationship with Jesus tend to feel like outsiders when they join us at Mass. The Mass doesn't make a whole lot of sense to them; it's puzzling, to say the least, and then there's all that standing and kneeling and sitting! We've found that if we help people fall in love with Christ and experience the power of the Holy Spirit, they want to come to Mass. This is true for our own people as well as for the unchurched, some of whom go on to become Catholic.

When we run Alpha as one more program among many, it becomes just another thing for our committed members to do, and it fails to accomplish its evangelistic goal. "I went on that retreat. I did Alpha. I did that Bible study." What we're trying to do, however, is help people discover their mission. That doesn't mean they'll go across the waters to foreign lands, although that might happen for some. It does mean that we will send them forth as disciples, reaching out to friends and family, where they work and where they play.

Thanks to Alpha, when the topic of faith comes up, people are equipped to speak with confidence about who God is and how he has changed them. And when parishes offer ongoing Alpha opportunities as part of a larger strategy, parishioners can invite those they encounter to investigate the topic of faith for themselves.

We've been running Alpha at Saint Benedict Parish for a long time, but this last season was our biggest yet. In my opinion, Alpha remains successful because we've used it to create a culture of invitation and have connected it to our pastoral plan. Our parishioners know Alpha isn't going away. They know that the culture of inviting those outside of the parish into a transformative relationship with Christ isn't going away. Ordinary, average Catholics are making a difference. They're bringing friends, family, and coworkers back to church and to a relationship with Jesus.

Guess what happens when people fall in love with Jesus? They come to church. They seek the sacraments!

When I arrived at Saint Benedict and began to work with Fr. James, we saw the bigger picture together. We could envision where Alpha fit within the larger scope of our parish's mission, and so we could be intentional about how to use Alpha and maximize its potential.

A while ago, I was approached by someone who was in charge of evangelization in his parish and wanted to use Alpha. I asked him where Alpha fit into his parish's plans, and he said they wanted to run Alpha to bring in the unchurched. As soon as Alpha was over, they'd move the participants into a Bible study. After the Bible study, they planned to run a series on the Theology of the Body. In their fourth year, they planned to put on a series by Fr. Raniero Cantalamessa that would take people deeply into the teachings of the Church. After they'd run a group through all of these programs in four years, they would start over again with Alpha.

I had to let this man know that there was a better way to accomplish their goal. By only doing Alpha every four years, they would miss out on making new disciples throughout the year, every year. Those other programs could help them establish well-informed disciples as part of a whole-parish strategy, but first and always they had to be making disciples. Alpha helps you make disciples.

Alpha and Our Game Plan

THE GAME PLAN

When we look at the Saint Benedict Game Plan—our pastoral strategy detailing how we form disciples who will joyfully live out the mission of Jesus Christ—we see the big picture. Our vision truly focuses on helping people enter a transformative relationship with Jesus Christ.

Early on we realized that we needed to support men and women who came through Alpha, to be in relationship with them and offer them opportunities that would nurture and strengthen them as they continued their journey into a relationship with Christ. Running Alpha without any follow-up is like offering someone the most incredible appetizer—a morsel of delicious food that promises a feast of epic proportions—and then escorting them out the door without ever getting to the main course. Alpha can become an isolated mountaintop experience. Without a bigger vision, the fire of a person's encounter with Jesus Christ can easily flicker and go out.

While Alpha is essential to our game plan, there are other key elements that help us live out our mission as a parish. After our people have completed Alpha, we invite them to become part of the Alpha team (more about this in the next chapter). There we continue to form them so that they can help others experience the beauty of Jesus in the power of the Holy Spirit through the Alpha process.

After people experience formation through their time on the Alpha team, we invite them to join a Connect Group—groups of twenty or so that gather regularly for a meal, a practical talk, fellowship, and prayers to help deepen their relationship with Christ. There, our parishioners can encourage and accompany people after they come through Alpha. Most parishes are too big to allow the pastor to give one-on-one support to every parishioner. The beauty of Connect Groups is that within them, people come to know and care for one another.

Some parishioners might have the gift of pastoring, a particularly useful gift for a Connect Group leader. I'm not referring to the canonical office of pastor but rather to a supernatural gift through which a person can help foster the spiritual growth of individuals. We are all gifted in some way (see I

Corinthians 12), and we want everyone in our church to use their gifts and serve in ministry—not because we want something from them but because we want something *for* them. As parishioners discover their gifts and put them in service to the Lord and his Church, they unlock a sense of their own purpose—the uniquely personal way they can participate in Christ's mission.

Along with our Connect Groups, we have Discipleship Groups that are designed to help parishioners grow in their understanding of the richness of our Catholic faith. Discipleship Groups help root people in the foundational disciplines of discipleship—prayer, reading Scripture, learning how to discern the will of God, applying the principles of the moral life to their own situations, and so on. The wells of our Church are deep.

The final icon in our game plan is worship. We think of Mass on Sunday as the highest form of worship because it is. But Alpha helps us see that there are other ways we can worship together. We pray together as staff, in our Connect Groups, in our youth groups, in individual encounters, and in virtually every group meeting or event. At its heart, worship is about offering to the Lord the praise and thanksgiving that he is due. It can take many forms: spontaneous prayer, singing, the Liturgy of the Hours, and other formal and informal prayers.

Worship helps people enter into a place where they're surrendering to Jesus. Surrender isn't a one-off deal. I don't know about you, but it's something I have to do over and over again. By creating a culture of worship, we give everyone a chance to constantly surrender to Jesus.

Our game plan illustrates our values, our beliefs, and the importance of situating Alpha within the parish's overall plan.

But I want to be clear: you don't need to have a perfect vision and plan in place before implementing Alpha. Fr. James and I didn't when we first came to Saint Benedict and decided to launch Alpha. We saw the Alpha process wake people up spiritually, but the gaps in our parish plan became evident as we tried to figure out what to do with all those newly awakened parishioners.

You might be thinking that we stopped doing Alpha until we had everything perfectly lined up. We didn't. We kept going. We knew the most important thing was bringing people to Christ, and our long-term plan for the church—our vision—came more sharply into focus as we went along. In fact, it wasn't until Year 4 of Alpha that we articulated our game plan.

Don't wait for the perfect plan before you start bringing people to faith. You can start Alpha and then develop the plan as you go, as long as you recognize from the start that Alpha is a small piece of that bigger puzzle.

Chapter Five

Alpha and the Leadership Pipeline

RON HUNTLEY

There's a crisis of leadership in our parishes, communities, businesses, and in politics. Pastors have—or have been given—the understanding that they carry the weight of the parish on their own. As a result, we have a prevailing culture that doesn't replicate leaders.

For too long we have labored under the mistaken idea that the pastor must be personally involved in every initiative, every discussion, and every facet of parish life. On the one hand, it's okay for people to help pastors execute their duties as leader— doing tasks from a list passed on "from above," for example, or shouldering part of the administrative load for "Father." On the other hand, at the end of the day, the parish looks to the pastor as the sole leader, the only person designated to move the community forward.

But "the function of leadership," according to Ralph Nader, "is to produce more leaders, not more followers."[16] By this standard, many parishes are failing. Parishes need leaders who, together with the pastor, are stewards of the parish vision—passionate about fostering that vision among members of the community and committed to its execution. Until we jettison the view of the pastor as some kind of super leader, we will continue to grind our priests under the weight of unrealistic expectations, and we will foster mediocrity in our parishes.

Alpha is a tremendous tool not only for forming disciples but also for raising up and forming leaders who can carry the vision, joyfully serve, and raise up others. We use Alpha this way at Saint Benedict: it functions as a powerful leadership pipeline for parishioners. In most churches, 20 percent of the volunteers do 80 percent of the work. This can lead to volunteer burnout and huge gaps in ministry. Alpha can address that issue by helping parishes raise up an army of volunteers: men and women who are not just random bodies filling gaps but competent collaborators. Furthermore, using Alpha in this way can help parishioners discover and begin to exercise their gifts. At Saint Benedict, we start this process by inviting some of the Alpha "alumni" to join the next Alpha team, where they are able to serve and we are able to mentor them.

As you think about Alpha as a leadership pipeline, keep in mind that you'll probably encounter three different kinds of volunteers: those who are primarily people oriented, those who are primarily task oriented, and those who are organizationally oriented. Roles like small group host, emcee, and speaker are natural fits for the people-oriented volunteers in your parish. Roles such as treasurer, member of the registration team, or member of the team that plans the Weekend Away are great for those who are more organization oriented. For those who are more task oriented, being on the kitchen team or the set-up team can be good fits. When I run Alpha, I want as many people as is appropriate to experience being part of the Alpha team. I look for opportunities to form the gifts of all three types of people, but in this chapter, we're going to focus on people-oriented roles.

Over the two to three years your parishioners serve on an Alpha team, you will draw them from one level of responsibility to the next, deepening and strengthening your parish culture.

Apprenticeship Culture

Before we talk about the specifics of using Alpha as a leadership pipeline, let's take a quick look at the culture of apprenticeship that we have established at Saint Benedict. A leadership pipeline depends on an apprenticeship culture. In the working world, an apprentice is someone who learns a skill or a trade by working for a time with someone who has the skills he needs. How do we apply that concept in parish life?

Well, the only way you can make your mission scalable, able to handle the requirements and demands of continued growth, is by raising up people who understand the mission, have a passion to serve, and have the skills to do what God is asking of them. At Saint Benedict, we form those kinds of people by bringing them through Alpha and then asking them to serve for a few seasons on Alpha in various team roles. In short, they serve an apprenticeship. As they serve alongside parish leaders, these leaders not only pass on skills but also model the behavior we want to see in emerging leaders as they are invited into roles of increasing influence and responsibility. This approach helps our leadership base grow.

We begin to specifically form our next team by Week 8 in an Alpha series. At that point, we pull the current Alpha team aside and ask them who at their tables would make good small group hosts for the next season (these hosts meet for discussion with the same guests for the course of the Alpha season). When we do this, we are looking for FACT people (see sidebar).

By the end of a season, we usually can sense whether or not a guest is faithful, available, contagious (is relatable to their peer group), and teachable. We can build on those characteristics and help them grow by inviting those people to join our next Alpha team. After a few seasons they leave our Alpha team, having been formed along the leadership pipeline that I'll describe, and they can be apprenticed in other ministries.

Roles for Small Groups

Let's get into the specifics of the Alpha team approach so that you can see how the concept of leadership development plays out.

Your guests are the most important people in your Alpha process. The second most important people are your Alpha team members. This team sits at the heart of your guests' Alpha experience as they meet over the weeks, get to know one another, and share meals and discussion. You've probably heard it said that an employee's experience of their company is only as good as its manager. We'd say that a guest's Alpha experience is only as good as your Alpha small group hosts are effective.

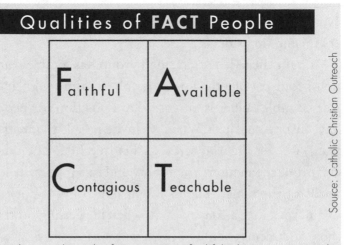

Qualities of FACT People

Faithful	**A**vailable
Contagious	**T**eachable

Source: Catholic Christian Outreach

Just a quick note about the first criterion: "faithful" doesn't necessarily mean faithful to the teaching of the Catholic Church. At first glance, that may seem shocking, but remember that our entire game plan is about helping others become disciples. That means walking with them on their journey, no matter where they are beginning. I have even invited hospitable, gifted atheists back to serve on the Alpha team, in hopes that their experience on the team would help draw them to Christ.

When we use the word "faithful" in the context of Alpha, we mean people who are going to be faithful to the concept and culture of Alpha. People who meet that criterion but who are not faithful in the ecclesial sense could be table helpers but not hosts or cohosts because those roles have more influence and require a higher degree of faithfulness to the Church..

The goal is to assemble a team that your non-Christian or unchurched best friend would be comfortable hanging out with for ten weeks. You have to know that you can trust your group host with anyone and that your guests will have an amazing experience. We don't ask for volunteers for an Alpha team. We recruit from our current guests through the evaluation and discernment of our current Alpha team—leaders raising up leaders.

At Saint Benedict, each small group has a table team made up of four people: the host, the cohost, and two helpers. The role of table helper is an entry-level position for people who have just taken Alpha. When we invite people to join the Alpha team, we ask them to serve in this role first. The table helpers' primary functions are to pray and to support the logistical needs of the table. Helpers might have opportunity to jump in and re-center a conversation when it's getting off track, but those comments should be brief, and the helpers should quickly make way for the guests to speak.

Observing how people handle their helper responsibilities and interact in the group enables us to identify those who have further capacity for leadership and who understand the purpose of Alpha. Why? Because we recognize that if people are too "big" to serve, then they are too small to lead. After their season as a helper ends, we can invite those humble helpers with leadership potential back as cohosts.

Cohosts act like helpers, but they are also available to stand in for the host when the host can't attend. If you see that the cohost excelled in the role and can carry even more responsibility, you can invite them back as a host for the next Alpha season.

The host facilitates the discussion and should be someone with a high level of emotional intelligence—a mature, socially aware person who can put guests at ease and isn't startled or offended by the sometimes very direct questions or gripes that guests have about Christianity and the Church. The host, as facilitator, knows when to let the conversation continue and has the ability to draw others into the discussion.

Also, a host knows how to avoid teaching during the small group discussion. Teaching happens in the Alpha videos that are part of each session, or a parish might present teaching in live talks. Small group discussion, on the other hand, is intended to be about the guests' thoughts and feelings regarding what they heard in the videos or talks, as well as their own personal experiences. (At Saint Benedict, meals and the video or talk take place at the tables, but small group discussion takes place away from the tables.) Alpha small groups are safe places for guests to express their hearts, perspectives, and beliefs. No teaching takes place in the discussion groups.

When we meet with our table teams for training prior to Alpha, we have found it inspiring to ask them to pray for the guests who will be sitting at their tables. We want them to visualize those empty seats filled with people, start praying for them, and continue praying for them as the sessions unfold. This keeps the Alpha experience saturated in prayer and helps the team to stay focused.

Selecting Your Small Group Hosts

When recruiting an Alpha table team, you might think that the logical first question is who to invite, but a better question is who *not* to invite. One type of person we tend not to invite is the Christian so exuberant in their faith that they don't know how to dial it back. Their way of speaking can be so steeped in piety that it's inaccessible or off-putting. Christians don't always realize that expressions that come naturally to us may sound like exclusive, insider language to others, creating a barrier that prevents guests from fully engaging in the Alpha experience.

When this sort of exuberant Christian is a host, I take them aside, invite them to be more aware of their overly religious language, and ask them to pull back in this area in order to help our unchurched guests respond to the process more freely. I point out that our goal is to help our guests share the joy of our faith and that we're walking with people who often come from a very different place. If, after having this conversation once or twice, the person can't find a way to speak at the other guests' level, then we won't consider them for future small group roles. There are other roles open to them, but being in a small group is just not one of them.

We also avoid inviting those who aren't sufficiently socially aware—people who ask awkward questions, for example, or fail to notice when their listeners have lost interest. These guests don't make great small group hosts: they're more likely to function as conversation stoppers than conversation start-ers. They have great intentions and beautiful hearts, but they don't have the emotional intelligence necessary to be a good Alpha table team member.

And we don't invite people who are in acute emotional pain. They may be suffering the loss of a loved one, the breakdown of a relationship, the loss of a job, or some other difficult life event. Guests often come to Alpha during such times because the setting gives them a chance to explore how God can be part of their lives during pain and crisis. Many times they experience amazing healings that give them a sense of peace and new pur-pose that can make them a great addition to the team. When we are considering which guests to invite to serve in table team roles, however, their brokenness, if not sufficiently healed, can be a problem if their need to be heard trumps their ability to listen. We want our table team members to be generous listeners, and if they are not in a space to be a good listener, then it isn't the right season for them to join our Alpha team as a host.

In a similar way, people with chronic unresolved issues or personality disorders tend to be ineffective hosts. Rather than having a temporary need to be heard, like those who are in acute crisis, these folks need to be heard at all times.

God has given everyone gifts and talents, and we try to find places for many guests to serve in small groups or other supporting roles. Some people, however, are just not in a healthy place yet to serve as a table team member. That does not exclude them in the future. People grow, change, and heal. It's not a judgment on anyone if we determine that they're better suited for roles other than those in which they'd directly accompany our Alpha guests.

Another thing: hospitality is a cornerstone for a successful Alpha small group; therefore, one trait we look for in all those who serve as hosts is a natural ability to put others at ease. In our experience, the Alpha small group that's laughing the most is the one that is not just having the most fun but most likely to bond and get the most out of Alpha. To that end, it helps if at least one table team member in every small group has the gifts and personality to "up the fun factor" for the small group. It's fine to have some serious people, but having at least one fun person in the group makes Alpha more enjoyable for guests.

We also try to balance the genders serving on each team, when possible. It doesn't matter if a man or a woman is in a particular role; what matters is who has the greatest capacity for the role. When we're building our tables, we also try to group our table team and their guests within ten years of age of one another. Having a shared cultural experience can make conversation flow more readily.

A final caveat: if you are new to Alpha as a parish, don't try to grow your Alpha opportunities faster than you can recruit great team members. You can be tempted to start with a massive Alpha guest group even though you only have one team member for each small group. Your eagerness to spread the gospel, however, will be upended by reality. You need to have a solid team for each small group; otherwise you're going to miss opportunities to reach your guests effectively as you build your Alpha culture. You only have one chance to make a first impression. If people have a bad Alpha experience, that is what they will share with others.

Continuing Formation

Once we have table teams in place, we don't just send them out to sink or swim. We have team meetings before each Alpha session, during which the team prays, and after each session, when the team debriefs what happened during that session.

We regularly remind team members of the Alpha principles: for example, that they are not supposed to teach. If a team member has in fact climbed on a soapbox, teaching and preaching during a session, the team can discuss this as a group in a constructive way. As the organizers, we can't be present at each small group conversation, so it's up to our table team to hold each other accountable for how they participate. Establishing this kind of accountability raises the likelihood that our guests have the space to share, without feeling overwhelmed by the team members. It also helps team members stay true to the principles of Alpha—to listen, accept, care for, and love the people in their group so that guests have the best experience possible.

We want to keep these team meetings fun and relevant. In these sessions, which essentially act as check-ins, we always thank team members for the commitment of their time and energy. We heap praise on people who are modeling the sort of leadership qualities and actions that are consistent with our parish's culture. When people feel appreciated and know that their contribution is noticed, it helps energize them and reinforces their desire to continue those behaviors.

Likewise, when a team member is struggling and perhaps seems unmotivated or spends time complaining, I pull them aside and try to help them problem-solve and elevate their attitude and their behavior. People who continue to be negative aren't invited back on the team because when we tolerate negativity it can drag the other team members down.

By praising positive leadership among your team members and nipping negativity in the bud, you are pruning the team so that they can bear more fruit. You're also working strategically to strengthen parish culture, because culture is created by what we reward and what we tolerate.

The way you interact with your team sets an example for them to follow. As you form team after team for your Alpha program, you create a culture in your parish. An expression famous in the business world is that "culture eats strategy for breakfast," but bad leadership eats culture for lunch! The people you bring through your leadership pipeline will be central to the parish culture you form. Be strategic in how you interact with your team and motivate them.

Selecting Your Alpha Emcee

If you want your guests to have a great Alpha experience, be on the lookout for an amazing emcee. There are four characteristics to keep in mind as you consider people for this role.

First, the emcee should be personable, have an engaging personality, and be able to put people at ease. Coming to Alpha can be intimidating, especially for unchurched guests but often for parishioners as well. It can take a lot of courage to show up for your first Alpha session. One of our parishioners, Bob, told me that he was invited to Alpha nine times and only decided to come the ninth time to get the lady that continued to invite him, Flavia, off his back. He was thrilled the learn the evening included wine and cheese. When he arrived, he fortified himself with some wine and then scouted out the exits for a quick getaway once the evening got rolling. Just before people were being invited to take a seat, when he was planning his getaway, Fr. James just happened to introduce himself, foiling his escape plan.

Choosing the right emcee can make the difference between a guest deciding to stay or deciding to leave. Let's take a simple thing, a joke, to illustrate how this can unfold. The emcee always starts Alpha by telling a joke, because laughter puts people at ease. Your emcee needs to be careful, however, to avoid inappropriate or insensitive jokes.

One of the best Alpha emcees I know had a joke about atheists that the team found hilarious when he tested it on them. It was a good joke on the surface, but I pointed out that it was probably going to alienate some of our guests, particularly considering that if we are doing Alpha well, we would hope to have atheists present. The fastest way to get someone out your door is to make them feel as if you brought them in just to make them the butt of your joke. It can feel like a schoolyard nightmare. By the way, that small bit of direction for an already excellent emcee helped him improve his service to the team and our guests, and it made him even more aware of the value of his ministry.

The second characteristic of a good emcee is positive presence—someone who is confident in who they are. If the emcee is nervous or ill at ease, everyone else in the room can feel it. The unease spreads faster than a cold in daycare.

Positive presence can be a two-edged sword, however. As the face of Alpha, emcees need to be team players first and foremost. But unlike the rest of the team, they are "on stage" and can be tempted to make it all about them. A good emcee, however, makes it about the guests. Part of the emcee's job in creating a good experience for the guests is to help keep things on track and have a firm idea about what to say even before showing up for the session. No inside banter or jokes please.

The third characteristic to look for in an emcee is youthfulness. If you don't have a young demographic at your parish, don't let that overwhelm you: youthfulness and age aren't always the same thing. If you want Alpha to be relevant to a younger demographic, however, you should try to have an emcee they can identify with and see as their peer.

My friend, Dave, who used to work at Ford, told me they had a saying: "You can sell an old man a young man's car, but you can't sell a young man an old man's car." When we put a young face at the front of the room, the older crowd are thrilled to see younger people leading. When we put an older face at the front, however, the younger crowd is more likely to feel as if they don't belong.

The fourth and most important characteristic is humility. The emcee needs to be able to work in a team and use the feedback from the team to improve from week to week. Remember, it's not about the emcee; it's about the guests.

It can take time to find the right emcee, but it's worth the effort. When I ran Alpha at another parish, I picked someone to be the emcee because he had presence; he was a very funny, personable, and an all-around great guy. I thought he'd do a wonderful job. But I also asked him because he struggled as a small group host: his background was in teaching, and he just couldn't resist teaching! I thought that making him an emcee would be a great way to benefit from his personality without putting him in a place where he would be teaching.

The more comfortable this man became as an emcee, unfortunately, the more he started to teach. No matter what I did, including making some big hand signals from the back when he started teaching, he just couldn't stop teaching. We ended up inviting him to serve in a different position on the team. There was no doubt that he was incredibly gifted, but he wasn't the right person for that role.

More recently I mentored someone to take on the role of emcee. At first he didn't seem entirely comfortable, but he grew into the role very quickly. He was spirited and helped the people in the room have fun and be comfortable. It was wonderful to watch him grow and blossom.

The biggest difference between the two emcees was that the second one was coachable. Being able to hear and accept feedback is what can make an acceptable emcee into a great one.

Finally, the emcee should know the flow of the evening, including the timing for each part of the schedule and the order in which different things need to happen. Putting a time sheet at the podium will help both rookie and seasoned emcees keep the evening running smoothly. Some emcees think that they can wing it, but lack of preparation is immediately obvious to the guests and sends a message that they're not a priority.

It sometimes happens that another obligation or an emergency disrupts the time the emcee has set aside to prepare. They shouldn't mention that from the podium. They should deliver the best they can and not apologize. Otherwise the emcee becomes the focus, distracting the guests.

Start with prayer when discerning who should be an emcee and look for the four qualities above. Sometimes the person you'd expect to excel doesn't work out, and the person who makes a rocky start ends up being exactly who you need.

Inviting People to Join Your Team

Before I tell you how to invite people to join your Alpha team, let me tell you how *not* to invite them. I know you're probably cringing as you read this, but don't invite people to join the team through a generic invitation: "Congratulations, you've been chosen . . ." or "We'd love to have you on our Alpha team . . ." Yes, that's what we used to do. Generic invitations do not work; they're not personal, and it's easy to say no to them.

Next we tried personalized invitations sent out by our task force coordinator. This wasn't effective either because our guests hadn't personally connected with the task force coordinator during their Alpha experience. Then we had our emcee (which was me at the time) personally invite people. This was a big improvement, but we still got a no from more than our fair share of people.

You can see where this is going. The most effective way to invite guests to join your Alpha team and have them say yes is to have their small group host personally invite them to join the team. We call it our "I see in you" conversation. After people say yes to their small group host, we send a follow-up email with an explanation of the level of commitment involved so that they can fully understand our expectations. As you're winding down one Alpha and transitioning to the next season, train your teams in how to make an effective invitation to the guests they've identified as potential team members.

Moving Team Members on from Alpha

Have you ever heard the tongue-in-cheek expression "You don't have to go home, but you can't stay here"? Well, that's an unofficial motto for our Alpha teams. "Hey, has Ron given you the boot yet?" we'll often hear our team members jokingly ask each other. We've done a good job making it clear that built into our leadership pipeline is the expectation that eventually our teams will move on from Alpha. Team members know that Alpha team is not a place to permanently pitch their tent. But remember, these experienced Alpha leaders have tremendous potential to take the training and formation they have received with Alpha into new ways to serve. How wonderful a blessing they can be to your church and the larger community once they leave the nest of the Alpha team!

As you move people along, it can help keep the pipeline flowing if you think of your teams according to three categories: new team, developing team, and graduating team. New team members are your first-timers, the people you're initiating into the Alpha pipeline of service and ministry. It's a time of enthusiasm and discovery for them, but it's also a time for those in senior leadership to use the FACT lens to identify future leaders. Developing team members are those returning to the team. They have some leadership experience that you're working to maximize as they move through various Alpha roles. Graduating team members are ready to move into other service in the life of the parish. The end goal for all three of these categories is to bring forward people who understand the vision for your parish and are actively engaged in its life.

It's important to get the conversation right when you're ready to move someone off the Alpha team. That talk can affect how they take their next steps after Alpha and should include some details and direction. Begin by thanking them for their commitment and generosity. Explain that you're moving them on because you need to make room for others to enjoy the benefits of being on the team. Ask them what types of things they have learned and how they have grown. Their answers will be a gift to you. Consider asking them to write down their answers so you can share them with others. Then let them know that their experience on the team has formed them to use their strengths to continue to build up the Church. Confirming and affirming that they have certain gifts gives them a sense of purpose as they go out to build the kingdom of God.

Talk about the importance of Connect Groups, and help them see that joining one is a priority so that their formation can continue. In a parish where you're forming many people, it's easy for some to get lost along the way. At Saint Benedict, Connect Groups are our way of making sure that as many as possible remain a part of our growing community.

In your conversation, make sure you cover these elements in a positive way, giving graduating members a sense of purpose. Also, ensure that you connect them with the right people, to get them engaged in appropriate ministries consistent with their gifts.

Alpha small group hosts have been formed firsthand in the art of listening and accompanying others on a journey toward Christ. As such, they could be tremendous assets in RCIA, for example, serving as a small group leader or sponsor. Youth ministry, young adult ministry, and discipleship groups might also be appropriate places for them, based on their personalities, strengths, and gifts. In addition, their ability to listen could bear fruit in places like bereavement ministry, visitation of the sick, prison ministry, or outreach to the poor. Basically, any ministry that requires someone to encounter another person and meet them where they are would benefit from their experience. It may be fruitful to pray with them and ask God to reveal to them the places of leadership and service he is calling them to.

During this conversation with graduating members, you will also have the opportunity to reflect with them on their Alpha experience—first as a guest and then on the Alpha team—and, most important, to thank them for their service, to ask for their prayers, and to encourage them to keep inviting their friends and acquaintances to Alpha.

At Saint Benedict, I have followed that conversation with an email to the pastor, sharing specifically how a graduating team member has been a gift through our Alpha seasons and affirming that they will be a gift to the parish. I copy the graduating team member on the email so that they see me celebrating them and their service. When Fr. James was the pastor, he replied with his thanks for their service as well. Essentially we want to let people know that we value them as individuals as they transition from Alpha team. This boosts their confidence as they move into other ministries and helps them stay connected with the parish after Alpha.

Sometimes you'll want graduating members to continue to be available to Alpha. When we encounter exceptional Alpha team members, we ask if they'd be willing to return to the team in the future if there's a need. It can happen that more people register for Alpha than we expect, and we don't have enough trained team members available. In those circumstances, we'll invite back graduated team members to help us, often on short notice. If we have guests drop out later, we can release these graduates from the team without concern that they will be offended or that it will affect their formation in the leadership pipeline. It's valuable to have a bull pen of people who you know are fully formed as Alpha leaders, ready to jump in when you need them. They become a true asset to your Alpha over the years.

I hope you can see the value of using your Alpha process as part of a leadership pipeline. It definitely requires intentionality, time, and effort, but the fruit is absolutely game changing in terms of parish culture and the mission of making disciples to which Christ has called us.

Chapter Six

Planning Alpha:
A Recipe for Success

RON HUNTLEY

As with any tool, you need to use Alpha well for maximum effectiveness. That requires thinking strategically about Alpha, planning appropriately and, as we have just discussed, recruiting intentionally. There's a famous saying: "God is in the details." Let's spend some time going through the details of planning, launching, and running Alpha so that it bears the most fruit in your parish.

Maybe you are already running Alpha and not getting the results you hoped for. Don't worry; it's not too late. Take a step back, use the information you find here, and reassess. I had to do something similar.

When I first started running Alpha, I was a member of a large parish in a big city. I identified some friendly, lively parishioners and invited them to my home to experience Alpha with me. I then invited those people back as a team to run Alpha. We launched Alpha for the entire parish and were able to run Alpha there for three seasons before I moved to a different province.

My new parish was in a small town, and most of the families had lived there for generations. For various reasons, the approach I had used in the city, with its frequent population turnover, wasn't a good fit here. We launched Alpha without really assessing our situation, however, and found that we primarily attracted people who were socially on the fringe of the community. They were wonderful people, but they didn't have the gifts needed to serve on the Alpha team. The people who did have the right gifts were in the pews on Sunday, but they weren't joining us for Alpha. In order to draw them in, we decided to focus on parents of young children for the next season.

This decision fundamentally changed our planning. We moved Alpha from Wednesday night to Friday night because most families were likely to be available that night. We decided to provide a fun-filled and engaging children's ministry that kids would want to attend. We knew that it would be easier for parents to come to Alpha if their kids wanted to be there too.

Finally, we renamed the evening Date Night Alpha. That name change reframed the whole event, making it more likely that young couples would take a chance on it. A date night filled with conversation with other adults, paired with an exciting and fun kids' ministry, was an easy sell. This strategy enabled us to present Alpha to people who we knew would have the gifts to contribute to the ongoing health of our Alpha process. Through those guests, we were able to reach out more effectively to the rest of the community.

Why do I bring this up? Because the first step in planning an Alpha involves deciding what kind of Alpha you want to run.

The Alpha organization offers three different video resources: Alpha with Nicky Gumbel, which features the popular speaker giving Alpha talks "live" from Holy Trinity Brompton Church in London; the Alpha film series, which contains the same content but uses multiple younger speakers in different locations across the world; and the Alpha Youth Series, which is similar to the Alpha film series but geared toward teens. Once you choose which video resource you want to use, you can narrow the focus and determine the "flavor" of your Alpha. We've hosted Youth Alpha, Family Friend/Date Night Alpha, Daytime Alpha for seniors, Alpha in restaurants and pubs, and a Morning Alpha designed specifically for young mothers.

It's important to consider which group you want to attract before you choose which resource you want to use. That decision will also affect your location, timing, the team you recruit, the music you play, and the food you serve. It will also help you determine if you need anything additional, such as children's ministry.

If you are interested in offering Alpha in your parish, you can find all the information you need to get started at alpha.org. With careful planning, the Alpha resources will help you bear fruit as you move ahead.

Let's drill down on the planning a little bit more.

Location, Location, Location

The adage "location, location, location" applies to more than real estate. Keep it in mind as you consider where to hold your Alpha sessions. As in real estate, there are benefits and drawbacks to whatever location you choose.

Many parishes opt to run Alpha at the church hall or in parish meeting rooms. Using parish facilities shows that you're putting evangelization at the heart of community life—a huge benefit. Familiarity with the facilities also creates an easier transition for guests who come to Christ and then want to join the community on Sunday for worship.

One of the drawbacks of holding Alpha at the parish is that some people aren't comfortable in a church setting. Fr. James often says that plenty of people have just enough experience of church to know they don't like it. Depending on your facilities, hosting it at the parish can present another drawback: many parish halls aren't very attractive. It's hard, but not impossible, to create a warm, hospitable feeling if the room design gives off a clinical or institutional vibe. You can mitigate that issue for Alpha sessions by having volunteers decorate the room to make it as inviting as possible.

You can also offer Alpha in the home, as I did when I first launched Alpha in my city parish. Alpha revolves around a meal, a movie, and conversation, and it feels comfortable to invite someone over to share those. The conversations that occur in the comfort of a home can be more natural and intimate—an added benefit. Parishioners can also find it easier to invite friends to their homes, knowing that their friends are already familiar with it and at ease there.

A drawback to running Alpha in the home is the difficulty in linking what's happening in the home with what's happening at the parish. (Regardless of where an Alpha course takes place, at Saint Benedict it is still parish-based, that is, under the umbrella of the parish.) It's possible for guests to transition from an Alpha run in the home to an engaged life in the church, but the path is not as obvious. If faith takes root, though, a guest will often ask team members where they go to church.

Unless a parish is careful, another drawback to hosting Alpha in a home is that it might not get the same level of support and resources available to Alpha sessions that take place in the church. To manage that, we make sure that no matter where we run Alpha, we offer the same training to every Alpha team. In addition, when we hold the celebration dinner at the end of the Alpha season, we invite all of the teams and their guests to attend, no matter the location of their Alpha sessions.

We have also found some success when we've offered Alpha in a pub or restaurant. As when running Alpha in a home, an obvious benefit to a restaurant or pub series is that it can draw in folks who would avoid attending something at a church. Another advantage of this location is that it doesn't require lots of setup, room decoration, or meal prep.

Some of the downsides include too much ambient noise and the possibility that the tables may not be large enough or may be too spread out. You may also find that, as in home-based Alpha, there isn't an obvious connection between the pub or restaurant and the life of the parish. We need to find ways to bring people to Christ, however, and if that means that the best option is to run Alpha while someone's drinking a beer and eating chicken wings, so be it.

We have even presented Alpha in the workplace. The benefit of running Alpha in the workplace is that people spend a great deal of time there and may be too busy working to ever attend an Alpha elsewhere. A few challenges to consider are that the videos are around thirty minutes long, so the small group discussion time will be much shorter if you want to finish in one hour. In addition, lunch breaks may not occur at the same time for everyone. As a result, people can end up moving in and out during a session, making it harder for trust to form and intimate conversations to happen. Despite those drawbacks, catching people at work may be the only opportunity we have to share with them the love, mercy, and forgiveness of the Father in Jesus Christ.

Based on our experience, we strongly recommend that you always run Alpha in the parish even if you are also offering it, in the same season, in different locations. Keeping the parish-based location front and center will help your parish see that evangelization is a priority for the community.

The same logic of "location, location, location" applies to your Weekend Away, which we discuss in chapter 9. The Alpha Weekend Away is a retreat focused on helping guests understand and experience the presence and power of the Holy Spirit. The preliminary question regarding this retreat is whether you choose to host it at your main Alpha location or somewhere else, such as a retreat center. We have learned that our guests are able to unwind, lower their defenses, and be more open to the rhythm of the weekend when we host the retreat somewhere other than our regular Alpha meeting space. Unfortunately, people can be reluctant to take a night or two away, and they sometimes find the cost a barrier.

Holding the weekend in your main location has benefits. It's easier to convince people to attend when they're already familiar with the location and also know that they can go home and sleep in their own beds each night. That said, when we present the weekend "in town," we usually have less time and need to run the videos at a pace that doesn't give our guests time to unwind, celebrate, and open up to the Holy Spirit. They end up consuming a lot of information, and some just watch the videos and then go home. That doesn't happen when we host the Weekend Away.

When guests stay overnight, they can move through the material at a more relaxed pace and, as a result, have a better overall experience. Even if we have lower numbers, the impact on our guests is much greater. When we make time for the Holy Spirit, he can work wonders.

Feeding Your Alpha Guests

Sharing a meal together is at the core of the Alpha experience because coming together for a meal helps build community. In Atlantic Canada, where Saint Benedict Parish is located, food is at the heart of our social gatherings. We're well-known for kitchen parties, where we share food, music, and dancing while we spin yarns in the kitchen. It's the most natural, friendly, and joyful experience. Strangers don't stay strangers for long in the warmth and welcome of a Maritime kitchen.

Alpha capitalizes on this human impulse to gather around a table for food: a generously sized warm meal is the first step to making our guests feel welcome and comfortable. The promise of a meal often gets people through the door who wouldn't normally come to an event like this, and it helps break the ice once they've joined us.

Needless to say, kitchen captain is a key role on the Alpha team. You need someone who not only knows their way around a kitchen but also is good with people: they'll be leading the team responsible for organizing and overseeing the meal, whether it is cooked on-site or not.

We've tried three models for providing a meal at Alpha: potluck, catering, and cooking the meal at church. Whatever model we use, we never impose a required fee, even if we ask for a freewill offering to help cover the expense. We don't want cost to be a barrier to a guest attending Alpha.

At a small Alpha we ran in a team member's home, the team provided the main course each week, and we asked our guests to bring the salads and desserts. This proved to be a very affordable model, especially for a small group. With a large Alpha, feeding guests can become more of a challenge, especially in terms of cost. Arranging a potluck might be the answer, but you risk the possibility that guests may not bring enough food or may not show up even when they have volunteered to provide part of the meal.

The first time we did a potluck, we realized that we didn't have enough food for the crowd. Panic ensued, and we got on the phone and ordered pizzas. We had to pull our team aside and tell them not to eat but, rather, to let the guests eat until the pizzas arrived. We learned from this experience to offset the risk of running short by asking people to bring more food than we might actually need, and we specify that the dish should serve ten or more.

Choosing the potluck model has other risks. Your Alpha guests might be younger and have little experience cooking for a crowd. More challenging, it can be a financial burden for them to buy the ingredients for a large meal. In addition, potlucks can become an added burden for female guests—whether they work outside the home or not—because they are disproportionately the cooks for their families. They can subconsciously associate their Alpha experience with added work, one more thing in an already overloaded week. We don't want anyone's Alpha experience to be tied up in negative feelings if we can help it.

Catering meals, on the other hand, frees up the kitchen team, who only have to serve and clean up, and it avoids the potential complications of a potluck. The obvious downside of catering is the cost, because you pay per predicted plate, regardless of who shows up. If you have a no-show, you're still on the hook for that meal. We keep attendance records over the years, and that gives us a good sense of trends regarding drops in numbers. This information makes it easier to budget for catering.

When we do cater, we often put a basket on the table for freewill offerings, with a suggested donation amount that will cover costs. You can also ask your emcee to invite people to donate whatever they are able. Historically we've found that we break even when we use this model.

A third and very cost-effective model is to have your kitchen team cook the meals in the church kitchen. When we choose this option, we give our team a budget, and they do all the shopping, prep work, cooking, and cleaning. Typically this brings the cost of the meal down to four or five dollars per plate. We put baskets at the table and invite people to give a seven-dollar donation—that three-dollar buffer covers those who can't pay, as well as our no-shows.

This model depends on establishing a capable team of skilled cooks who can prepare a meal for a large crowd on a tight schedule. That difficulty, however, is balanced by the wonderful opportunity to build up people who have these gifts and are ready to use them as part of a team.

It doesn't matter what your budget is or how many team members you have in the kitchen. There's a model that will work for you so that you can gather your guests around a meal as you bring them closer to Christ.

Operations: Details Matter!

You don't get a second chance to make a first impression. Without an effective operations plan and the right people executing that plan, your Alpha can fall apart, closing someone off to further conversation about Jesus. Something as simple as testing the audio-visual equipment and making sure microphones have fresh batteries can help the evening run seamlessly.

To facilitate smooth operations, you'll need to put together a checklist of critical items needed for the evening and duties related to operating or overseeing equipment, setting up tables and chairs for the event, and so forth. Delegate someone with the appropriate skills to be responsible for managing that list. They and their team members will do everything from making sure the video equipment is in place to checking that sight lines to the screen and podium are clear from every table.

These things should all be done ahead of time. You don't want to give your guests the impression that you're scrambling around at the last minute. Preparation, organization, and good execution show our guests that they are important to us.

From a guest's perspective, good operations start with the on-site registration. (At Saint Benedict, people can register ahead at our parish website or when they arrive, using a paper form.) How they experience registration on the first night sets the tone for the rest of the Alpha process. Therefore, when we do on-site registration, we want to make sure the process is seamless. We want guests to come in, feel welcome, and be easily walked through the process so that they can fully enter into the Alpha experience.

The registration form should ask only for the information you need and explain clearly how you will use it. If you're tracking demographics, including how they heard about Alpha, it's best to ask them those questions up front. If you're seating people at tables based on approximate ages, you need to make sure you have an age-range category on the form. Creating a registration form that helps you collect data effectively can help you improve your planning and also help give your Alpha guests an experience tailored to their needs.

Budget planning is one of the most significant operational issues and is critical to running a smooth Alpha. Build the budget, know who has the authority to approve that budget, and aim to break even. Asking your guests to donate for meals can help with immediate costs, but you may also need to invest in curtains and other decorative items, sound equipment, or kitchen supplies. Build a comprehensive budget that includes all of your costs, and have it approved ahead of time.

Creating a Welcoming Environment

A welcoming environment will go a long way toward helping people feel comfortable and easing the tension some will feel about attending Alpha. Even simple gestures can make a difference. Alpha team members can welcome guests at the door every night, help them find their tables, offer to take their coats, fill their water glasses at the table—in general, treat them as they would guests in their own homes. Alpha guests will appreciate this radical hospitality. It's something, sadly, that people rarely equate with coming to church.

In whatever venue we're holding Alpha, we try to make the physical space welcoming too. At Saint Benedict, we've invested in nice tablecloths and battery-operated candles to create a warm ambience and to help dress up our otherwise bland parish hall. One of our Divine Renovation Network parishes included new curtains and wall paint for their hall in their Alpha budget. Another network parish brought in fresh-cut flowers for their tables. Yet another parish had Alpha mugs made, used them for their coffee service over the course of the program, and then sent one home with each guest at the end of their Alpha experience.

At Saint Benedict, we also give some thought to music when we consider the overall atmosphere we want to create. We play secular music in the background as our guests arrive and while we share a meal. It's a subtle thing, but it sets people at ease—especially the unchurched, who might be put off by "churchy" music, no matter how softly it's playing.

These details might not seem any different from what you do to prepare for guests in your own home—and that is exactly the point. Alpha guests are truly God's gift to us, and we want to do everything we can to help them experience love and hospitality. Paying attention to the details will help create the kind of atmosphere that will bear great fruit.

Chapter Seven

Issues and Impact

RON HUNTLEY

We are committed to excellence in ministry at Saint Benedict Parish. That same commitment is a part of the fabric of the Divine Renovation Network. We believe that executing well the things that God asks us to do honors him and respects the dignity of the people we serve. It's about offering to the Lord our firstfruits—the very best that we can give. Excellence in ministry also helps remove obstacles that people might have to accepting and cooperating with the grace of God.

In Alpha we pursue excellence by offering all participants—especially our guests—the best experience we possibly can. In order to do that, we have to be rigorously candid with ourselves, courageously respond to issues when they come up, and embrace continuous improvement.

We've discussed how hosts meet regularly during Alpha to reflect on how well they are serving guests. Their goal is to make each guest's experience a positive one, but sometimes the guests themselves make that difficult. It is up to the Alpha team to deal with situations directly and compassionately so that they don't negatively affect the Alpha experience for the rest of the guests.

No-Shows, Late Arrivals, and Those Who Quit

Three of the most common issues that can present obstacles in an Alpha season are no-shows, chronic late arrivals, and guests who quit Alpha. It's good to be prepared for these possibilities emotionally, psychologically, and operationally.

On the surface, no-shows don't seem like a big problem. But when you've put a lot of planning into the makeup of each table, no-shows leave gaps and can throw off the table "balance." As previously noted, we keep statistics from our Alpha program each season, which help us track trends—including the average percentage of no-shows. Over time, we have discovered some ways to mitigate this issue.

For example, we host an Alpha Celebration Event at the end of each Alpha season so that our guests can close out their experience with a party. We encourage them to invite their friends and family to this event. This allows them to share that experience with those close to them, and we often get a number of our next season's sign-ups at this celebration. We discovered that sometimes the potential guests forget about Alpha because of the gap between when they sign up and when the next season starts; it just slips their minds. So we learned to set up a reminder process.

To jog their memory, we send all our new Alpha guests an email two weeks before the season launches. This also gives guests who signed up but can no longer make the commitment an opportunity to let us know. An added benefit is that we're able to find out if there were errors in email addresses during the sign-up process. E-mailing people two weeks before gives us time to follow up with a phone call to reissue the invitation if their email bounces.

On one occasion when I was calling guests whose emails had bounced, I connected with Richard, who said he didn't recall signing up. He was a person of integrity and wanted to honor a commitment that he had made, but he went on to explain that he was unsure about this Alpha thing. With all the scandals that had plagued the Church, he had lost heart with the Catholic Church. He told me that he would attend Alpha to fulfill the obligation, but then he was likely going to stop coming to church.

I felt tremendous empathy for him. My world had been rocked by the scandal in the Church too, and I told him as much. I let him know that I thought he'd really enjoy Alpha, and that if after attending the sessions he still didn't want to attend church, I would understand.

In the end, Richard was renewed through the Alpha process and continued coming to church every week. He is now a dear friend. He joined us on the Alpha team and moved through the leadership pipeline. He is a wonderful disciple of Jesus Christ and now helps us run a prison Alpha program with others from his parish. He has also gone on a parish mission trip to Chile to build a school and to establish Alpha locally. If we hadn't followed up with something as simple as a phone call, we would have missed the opportunity to bring him closer to Christ. Don't underestimate the power of an email or phone call to reinvite guests for your upcoming season!

Chronically late guests present another issue. I must be honest and say that initially I was judgmental and maybe even a little annoyed with guests who regularly showed up late. It took me some time before I understood that, as a follower of Christ, my first response should be compassion. A guest's chronic lateness presents an opportunity for us to enter into their life in a helping way. Often there is a real issue behind their lateness—an issue we might be able to solve.

For example, a guest might take public transportation and can't arrive sooner, but we might have a team member who could pick them up. Some guests choose to come late because the food we're serving doesn't fit their dietary needs. Knowing that, we can easily arrange to have food available that they can eat. If we enter into judgment and don't ask questions to help us get to the reasons behind a problem, we can't address the problem.

We had a young guest who arrived late every single week. When our team asked her about it, she apologized and said that her work schedule wouldn't allow her to come any earlier. To help her have the best Alpha experience possible, from then on the team made sure to have a hot meal ready for her when she arrived. When Alpha was over, she testified that their attention and care for her helped open her heart to the Lord. Sometimes we can find a solution that will help a guest arrive on time, but when we can't, as with this young woman, we make sure we take care of them.

One of the most disappointing moments in Alpha is when guests quit. No matter how long our guests spend with us, I can't help but grow to love them. I want them to experience Alpha because I know that it creates opportunities to meet Jesus. Yet for various reasons, some people quit. It always breaks my heart.

At the start of every season, we encourage people to attend three times before they decide to stop coming. That gives them time to get a real sense of what Alpha is and to develop relationships before they decide it's not for them. This simple invitation to give it a try has helped decrease the early dropouts.

Sometimes, even with that extra encouragement to keep coming, we have a drop-off right at the beginning. This can lead to difficulties for the small groups we've set up. When we're only a few weeks in and we have four hosts and only two guests, we need to decide if we want to combine them with another table or keep the group going as it is. There isn't a perfect answer. Sometimes those tables shrink and grow week to week, and it can be a real challenge to figure out how to handle the flux.

In Alpha, we don't chase people down when they stop coming. That approach is a central Alpha value but, obviously, there is a real difference between not chasing people down and not caring about them. And so at Week 3, our small group hosts invite their guests to share their email addresses and phone numbers with them so that they can keep in touch throughout the Alpha experience. The registration team has that information, of course, but we don't presume our guests want others in the parish to use them; hence the personal request. Having the contact information allows team members—after the three-week mark—to reach out via an email, text, or phone call to guests who have missed a week or two to make sure that they're okay and to let them know we're looking forward to seeing them the next week.

People who drop out before three weeks don't receive emails asking them how they are. It could feel as if we're hassling them rather than checking on a friend. We need to be true to our word and our values, and if we say we're not going to chase them down, then we shouldn't.

Each of these three situations—no-shows, late arrivals, and dropouts—can be discouraging and challenging for your operations, but don't give up. If you keep track of your registrations and then examine statistics over time, you can use them to identify patterns, come up with possible solutions, and train your team to know what to expect.

Managing a Difficult Guest

This may seem like semantics, but there's actually no such thing as a difficult guest—only guests who put us in difficult situations. Alpha attracts a range of personalities, and that's part of its genius. It also means that we need to find ways to ensure that *all* of our guests have as positive an experience as possible—even the ones who make things more challenging for us. If we can do this, we will create opportunities for them to have a transformational experience through Alpha.

One type of guest who can diminish a small group's experience is the over-talker. This person dominates the conversation and doesn't give fellow guests the opportunity to share. Dealing with this situation tactfully can be awkward.

The host's easiest approach is usually to thank the guest for their perspective and then ask other guests to share. This redirection gives others the opportunity to break into the conversation without embarrassing that guest. If the guest continues to dominate the conversation as time goes on, we often find that we need to pull that guest aside, thank them for their zeal, and ask them to help us draw out the other people in the group.

By gently making them aware that other guests aren't sharing, the over-talking guest can become an ally to the team. They may find this difficult, but it's a growth opportunity for them.

Interrupting a guest, cutting them off, or stating out loud that they're talking too much will drive them away. By using subtle redirection or enlisting them to ensure that others speak, we end up addressing the situation without any embarrassment.

On the flip side, there's the guest who doesn't share at all. It's easy to perceive their silence as a sign that they're not engaging with the material, but that might not be the case at all. It's important to give everyone a space to share, but some people learn better by listening. Even though they're quiet, they're very engaged.

I find that this situation is more likely to make *me* uncomfortable than it does the guest. The best way to manage it is to continue to invite everyone to share and to make room for silence in the discussion. Those moments of silence can help people process their thoughts before they speak. Some guests think while they're talking, but others need to fully process what they are thinking before they contribute. We try to keep in mind the fact that we're dealing with different personalities.

We've already discussed another type of guest who presents a difficult situation: the overzealous Christian or "uber-Catholic" who uses churchy or pious language. Our emcee tries to preemptively deal with this situation by reminding our guests at the beginning of Alpha that we should dial back on religious jargon for the sake of others. Despite that, we occasionally find that some guests don't get the message.

Our small group hosts sometimes address this situation by asking the guest what they mean by specific terms. This can help alert them to the fact that their language is excluding others, and it gives them the opportunity to rephrase what they've said. If they continue to use religious jargon, our hosts pull them aside for a conversation. Team members make it clear that they're not criticizing the guest's faithfulness, just pointing out that their religious jargon is a barrier to encountering Christ for others in the group.

Most guests respond well to these conversations. They understand that we're enlisting them in the cause of evangelization. They want their fellow guests to have the type of experience that will bring them into a relationship with Christ, and they may not even be aware of how much exclusive language they use. Even if we need to do some minor corrections as the weeks go on, these guests tend to dial back because they are passionate about making opportunities for God to work through Alpha.

Occasionally we encounter aggressive guests who are antagonistic to the faith. Although this may seem like a nightmare to some people, I look forward to this situation. Much of the time, aggressive guests are testing whether we will judge them or tell them what to believe.

I heard an Alpha story that took place in prison. One of the guests was a hardened and violent criminal. The man shared that he came from an abusive environment and that wanted to be feared. He deliberately acted as violently and crazily as he could, which led to plenty of time in solitary confinement. When he was first invited to come to Alpha by an inmate delivering magazines, he threatened to knock the guy out and chased him away. Despite the initial response, the inmate invited him again—but not before placing the mail cart between them. He then moved quickly and shouted, "Alpha starts tonight at 7 p.m., and there's going to be food!" and kept going.

Apparently, in prison extra food was used as an incentive, so this guy decided that he would go for the food and cause as much trouble as possible. Nuns from the community were running Alpha, but that didn't stop him from going through with his plan. He humiliated them and talked down to them. He was arrogant, disruptive, and cruel to these women every single week—and every single week the nuns loved him. He gave them every reason in the world to kick him out. They didn't. They listened, and they loved him. As Alpha was ending, he asked them why they had endured it all. They said, "We love you, and God loves you."

He went back to his cell that night and said, "Jesus, I hate myself. I am not a good man. If you are real, please show me and help me because I am so alone." He went on to share that he felt the love of God flow through him. He cried for the first since he was a young boy, until he fell asleep. When he woke up the next day he felt different. "Everyone else saw it too," he testified. "Jesus changed my life."

When I encounter a guest who's antagonistic or aggressive, I thank God. That's exactly why we do Alpha—to reach those who are broken and hurting. I encourage you to be patient with those people and to love them.

Inviting Guests Off Alpha

In my nineteen years running Alpha, I've only had to invite one guest to leave. It rarely happens, but it's important to prepare for that conversation so that you can do it well.

The truth is that Alpha isn't a great fit for everyone. The two types of people who are most challenging are those who show up with an axe to grind and those who are overzealous about their religion (as opposed to simply using religious jargon unthinkingly). In both cases, they are difficult to manage as guests because they are focused entirely on their own agenda.

We work to empower small group hosts to interact positively with these guests and share with them how their behavior affects other guests. Most times those conversations go very well, but occasionally they don't, and guests conclude on their own that Alpha isn't for them. We're always sad when our guests don't return, but we understand that if people can't modify their behavior to ensure that everyone has a positive experience, then it's true—Alpha isn't for them. We'd rather see a good but overzealous Catholic leave the Alpha process than see a guest from outside the Church have a bad experience.

People with an axe to grind are the other challenging group. The person I had to disinvite had an axe to grind about a specific denomination. On the first night of Alpha, this person dominated the group conversation, pursuing this issue. I redirected the conversation several times and invited other guests to share, but this guest insisted on bringing the discussion back to his issue.

I could tell that the rest of the group was quite upset. At the end of the night, three guests approached me and said they wouldn't come back if this was how the discussion was going to go. That was a reasonable response to the other guest's persistent behavior. I knew I was going to have to have a conversation with that man before the next session. He did not show up the following week, so I figured I was off the hook.

The next session, this guest showed up while we were eating. I quickly got up from my table, took him aside, thanked him for coming back, and let him know I was looking forward to getting to know him. I said that I hoped he felt he had had adequate time to fully air his issue in that first week. I then expressed my hope that this issue wouldn't keep resurfacing, because it made the other guests feel ill at ease.

His response shocked me. He said that as a guest, he would do whatever he wanted and say whatever he wanted for as long as he wanted. Obviously, this wasn't going to work for his fellow guests, who had come for the Alpha experience, not to listen to him grandstand. I invited him again to join us and enter into the spirit of what we were doing. If he could stay focused on the material we were presenting and give other guests the opportunity to speak, he would be more than welcome.

He again resisted and said we couldn't kick him off Alpha. I told him that I wasn't kicking him off but giving him a clear understanding that he needed to participate in a way that respected the other guests. If he was choosing not to participate in that way, then he was self-selecting to leave Alpha. He ended up leaving and writing a letter to our pastor, our bishop, and probably the pope too.

We can't let one person dictate everyone else's experience. When a guest does that, you have an obligation to be open and honest with them about how their behavior impacts everyone else. That conversation will lead to the guest either modifying the behavior, choosing to leave, or trying to stay without changing what they're doing. In the latter case, you'll have to invite them to leave in order for the other guests to have a good experience.

After-Alpha Assessment

Forming teams, welcoming guests, paying attention to the details, sharing food, learning how to care for challenging guests—all these are essential elements of Alpha. It's just as important to conduct a post-Alpha evaluation after each season so that you can improve and better serve your guests. We collect data through our registration form at the beginning of Alpha, and we also collect data at the end of each season. We direct our guests to a free online survey site, where we have posted ten questions designed to help us determine the value Alpha is bringing to our parish culture, its impact on our guests, and what we can do to improve.

Here's an example of one of our surveys:

1. How did you hear about this Alpha course?
   a. Coworker
   b. Neighbor
   c. Family member
   d. Friend
   e. At church
   f. Website
   g. Electronic sign at church

2. Why did you decide to take Alpha at this time in your life?
   a. Personal change had me asking questions and seeking answers where I had not looked before.
   b. I saw positive change in the person who invited me, and I had to check it out.

c. I figure that there must be more to life than this! So I invested some time in Alpha.

d. People seem really excited about Alpha, so why not?

e. Because I was asked by someone I trust.

f. I am curious about issues of faith, and the timing was right.

g. No idea really; it just happened.

3. When it comes to matters of Christianity, I would say that before taking Alpha, my attitude was

a. adversarial. I disliked the topic and had little positive to say about it.

b. apathetic. It was just not something I was personally concerned with one way or the other.

c. I got the "God" thing, but the rest was unclear (for example, Jesus or the Holy Spirit).

d. I was a Christian but with no real experience of Jesus or the Holy Spirit.

e. I was a Christian but with no real relationship with Jesus that led to joy and enthusiasm.

f. I was a Christian in need of being refilled and reinspired.

g. I was a solid Christian who enjoyed walking with Jesus by the power of the Holy Spirit.

4. Now that I have completed the Alpha experience, I would say my faith has

a. gotten weaker. This was not helpful.

b. remained the same. No change one way or the other.

c. grown—which was fun and helpful.

    d. taken on new importance and is starting to give my life more purpose.

    e. come alive in ways I could only dream of. This is awesome!

5. What was your experience with the Church before your Alpha experience?

    a. Hostile—critical nonattender.

    b. Indifferent—nonattender.

    c. Wanted to attend but had just drifted away.

    d. Indifferent attender—not engaged.

    e. Regular attender and active—yet was not comfortable sharing my faith.

    f. Committed member who was comfortable sharing my faith.

6. Where would you say you are now with respect to your relationship with the Church?

    a. I am still a hostile and critical nonattender.

    b. I am still an indifferent nonattender.

    c. I am content attending and not getting engaged in the life of the Church.

    d. I plan to start going to church and seeing what happens.

    e. My experience of church is being enriched, and I plan to be involved.

    f. I love being a part of the Church and will continue with joy.

7. Did you attend the Holy Spirit retreat?
   a. No, I was not interested at all.
   b. No, it did not feel right to go at the time I was asked to commit.
   c. No, I wanted to but could not make it.
   d. No, I was signed up, but something came up and I had to cancel.
   e. Yes.

7. Before your Alpha experience, would you have invited people to something faith-based?
   a. No
   b. Yes

8. After your Alpha experience, would you invite someone to something faith-based, like Alpha?
   a. No
   b. I just may now.
   c. Yes

9. In which of the following ways would you be open to following up your Alpha experience?
   a. Going back to my faith or church of origin and reconnecting.
   b. Committing or recommitting to reading the Bible.
   c. Committing or recommitting to taking time for daily prayer.
   d. Taking a follow-up program like Catholicism 201, Dogmatic Theology, Bible Study, etc.
   e. Helping on an evening Alpha team.

f. Helping on a daytime Alpha team.

g. Trying out a Connect Group.

h. Reconnecting with my Alpha small group friends.

i. Becoming a member of Saint Benedict Parish.

j. Becoming a Catholic.

We ask the first question (How did you hear about this Alpha course?) to determine how to reach the greatest number of people most effectively. When we are getting set to run a new Alpha season, we don't just put an announcement in the bulletin. Most people come to Alpha because of a personal invitation, and so we encourage people to invite, invite, invite. The answers we get back on the surveys always affirm that a personal invitation gets the best results.

We ask question 2 (Why did you decide to take Alpha at this time in your life?) because it helps us understand the forces in a person's life that make them more open to accepting the invitation to join us. If we can understand why people say yes, we can educate our parishioners to watch for these moments in people's lives, knowing they are prime times to invite them to Alpha. This is also a great indication of when the best time might be to reinvite someone who said no before.

Questions 3 and 4 (attitudes towards Christianity and faith before and after taking Alpha) help us identify how hearts have been moved and changed through the Alpha experience. This is also a great way to identify our Alpha witnesses for the next season. People who were hostile to Christianity or disengaged and then experienced a transformation through Alpha can often speak powerfully of their experience to others. In a similar way, questions 5 and 6 (experience of the

Church before and after Alpha) identify changes in attitude in relation to the Church.

Question 7, regarding whether the guest attended our Holy Spirit retreat, is useful for planning purposes and helps identify the barriers people face in joining us. Questions 8 and 9, which ask if the guest has invited people to faith-based events in the past and would after taking Alpha, present another opportunity to understand how people experience Alpha. Finally we use question 10 (ways to follow up on the Alpha experience) to help us determine areas of interest for our guests and consider some ways for them to get more involved in the life of the parish.

Collecting the hard data through a simple survey like this can help you measure and affirm the impact that Alpha is having in your parish. It can also help you identify where guests might best use their gifts as they come through the leadership pipeline.

Scaling Alpha

When it comes to Alpha, you can only start where you are, right now, as a parish. But don't let small thinking place artificial limits on what God wants to do through your Alpha initiative. If you strive to provide your guests with the best possible experience by finding the right people to serve on the Alpha team, assess your progress as you go, and evaluate your impact after each season, chances are that your Alpha process will continue to grow. It's always good to begin with the end in mind, however, and so I want to present three different possibilities for how you can scale Alpha—that is, let it serve more people.

The first way—I think of it as organic growth—involves identifying people with capacity for leadership and investing in them. This is essentially how we started at Saint Benedict. Talk to these people about the potential and gifts you see in them, and invite them to commit to and grow by being part of your Alpha team. You will be mentoring them, and they in turn will mentor others later. As you form more leaders, you will grow big enough to accommodate the number of guests you want to reach every Alpha season. You'll then be able to move fully formed leaders into other ministries, as we've discussed, for the maximum impact on growing the kingdom.

Another way to maximize your Alpha impact is to branch out. In other words, keep running Alpha at your parish building but also provide satellite Alpha experiences elsewhere, as we discussed in chapter 6. One parishioner wanted a very dear friend to take Alpha, but her friend wasn't comfortable coming to the church. We invited the parishioner to lead Alpha in her own home. She had worked her way through the leadership pipeline and fully understood the culture of Alpha, so this was easy for her to do. We empowered her to take it to the people she loved.

Another parishioner was a business owner who wanted to share Alpha with his employees but knew that he couldn't bring them to the parish. He chose to run Alpha at work. Again, he was prepared to take on that challenge because he was fully formed through the leadership pipeline. In the same way, a team of parishioners has taken Alpha to a prison. We've even been approached to take Alpha to a CrossFit setting (a gym)! When you raise up leaders and equip them, they can make

Alpha a powerful outreach to the world in a seemingly endless variety of ways.

The third way to scale Alpha is through what we can think of as "missionary" outreach. Other parishes and communities are going to hear about what's happening at your parish and come knocking, asking questions about Alpha. I hope you will be as generous as possible in helping them.

Sometimes communities don't feel they have the resources to get Alpha off the ground. When that's happened in our area, we have missioned a group of our own Alpha team members to go into that parish and help them get Alpha going. Over a season or two, as the host community builds up its own Alpha leaders, we're able to pull out our team. We're happy to offer this help because we're eager to perpetuate a culture of evangelization through Alpha.

When it comes to Alpha, you need to always think about scaling. Don't be limited by the size of the Alpha course you had when you started. Know that God wants to use you not only to grow Alpha and the culture of evangelization in your parish but also to export it to other venues and bless other communities if invited. Remember, this isn't just about revitalizing your community; it's about living the mission of the Church.

Chapter Eight

Promoting Alpha

RON HUNTLEY AND FR. JAMES MALLON

Ron

When the time comes to promote Alpha, you will find excellent videos and marketing material online at the Alpha website. You can use a full array of approaches, from e-mailing parishioners and putting announcements in the bulletin (the most basic levels of promotion) to social media, flyers, billboards, newspaper ads, signs outside the church, and so on. All these efforts, however, are merely means to support the most effective method for bringing people to Alpha: personal invitation. As previously noted, our surveys unfailingly demonstrate that personal invitation is the single most important factor in bringing a person to Alpha and helping them stay.

It can be scary for parishioners to step out and invite someone. Catholics aren't in the habit of inviting people to seek a relationship with Christ. When parishioners understand what Alpha is, however, and when they have experienced it themselves, they're excited and more open to making an invitation.

A key factor here is expanding people's vision regarding what constitutes a mission field. At Saint Benedict, we work hard to help our people see that every encounter with another person takes place in a "mission field." Where we work, where we socialize, where our kids hang out, our neighborhood—all of these are mission territory. Understanding this helps break down the artificial wall that many Catholics build between their "church" life and their "real" life, and it makes it easier for them to reach out to others.

Over the years we have found that for every five people we invite to Alpha, one person will actually come. So you can see that if invitations are the prime means for bringing people to Alpha, you have to do a lot of inviting. We challenge each of our parishioners, every season, to personally invite five people to try Alpha.

One of the parishes in the Divine Renovation Network took an innovative approach and combined personal invitation with traditional promotion. They created a postcard-sized invitation listing Christmas activities and Mass times. On the reverse side, they ran an invitation to their upcoming Alpha. Their parishioners hand delivered twenty thousand of these invitations! The personal contact, along with the physical reminder of the upcoming events, was especially important in the neighborhood around the church. The proximity increased the chances that some of these neighbors would connect with the parish through Alpha.

In order to support this culture of invitation, you'll need to pray and ask God to send you people to invite. As the invitations start rolling out, celebrate them regardless of the result. Have a competition on your staff to see who can invite the most people. Collect stories from your parishioners about their efforts to invite people, and ask your priests and deacons to include some of those stories in their homilies. Celebrating in this way emphasizes the kind of culture you want to create in your parish and makes it less intimidating for the person in the pew to issue an invitation. If Fr. Simon Lobo can invite a stranger he met while biking and someone he met on a flight, and Fr. James Mallon can invite his physiotherapist, as both of them did, then I can invite my cousin, my coworker, or my friend.

One of our Divine Renovation Network parishes launched Alpha this year after working hard to educate their parishioners about the process. The parishioners were excited, and the Alpha staff told them that they were more than welcome to come. If they were going to attend, however, the price of admission was to bring a guest. As a result, over two hundred people signed up for their very first Alpha. One hundred people came to Alpha who weren't connected with a church because someone took the initiative to invite them! Can you imagine what that's going to do to ignite that parish?

Getting Your Parishioners to Invite

Fr. James

Saint Benedict recently had the largest Alpha group it has seen so far, with a high percentage of guests being unchurched. When I was pastor at the parish, people often asked me where we found all these new people, twice a year, for Alpha. Did we put up signs or advertise? Yes, but as Ron has emphasized, invitations from parishioners were and continue to be the most successful and effective outreach.

This is especially true when it comes to bringing in the unchurched. We all have people in our lives who are not connected to church or who aren't believers. The genius of Alpha is that for the Catholic who wants to evangelize, it's like "evangelization for dummies." It doesn't require a lot of elaborate personal preparation or an extensive time commitment. It's as easy as inviting someone to come and share a meal.

Invitations will only happen in your church if you've grown an invitational culture. I'd like to offer some thoughts about this from a pastor's perspective because the pastor plays a key role in fostering that invitational culture. If the pastor is on board, then he can help make it the norm for parishioners to invite the unchurched to an encounter with Christ in Alpha. To this end, the pastor should communicate from the pulpit why Alpha is a powerful tool for raising up disciples and why, in that capacity, it is not just one program among many.

Over the years, people have remarked on my preference for Alpha over other ministries, and I don't disagree. Alpha earns pride of place by the nature of what it can accomplish in the most outward-looking manner. It helps people encounter Jesus in a life-changing way better than any other ministry or program I have used. It brings them into a relationship with Christ while also offering an incredibly effective means to begin to disciple those already in the Church and to raise them up as leaders. Any ministry that can do all of that is automatically my favorite ministry.

If you are a pastor, you need to decide the role Alpha will play in your parish. If you envision a significant role for Alpha, you need to take ownership of that vision. You will then be able to communicate to your parish the potential long-term impact you hope to have using Alpha.

When I've served in a parish, I have made it a point to be very involved in Alpha. I made sure I was part of the training. I was often the emcee or a small group host. You can't ask parishioners to make the commitment to Alpha unless you, as the pastor, personally commit to it yourself. When you demonstrate your personal commitment to this tool, you impress upon the parish its significance and value. Now this certainly does not mean the pastor has to do everything. In fact, we should seek every opportunity to empower our Alpha team to utilize their gifts. If, however, they get that chance to see just how committed we are to Alpha, it will encourage them and all of our parishioners to really lean into the experience.

When you've made that commitment, you can convincingly promote Alpha to your people. If you and your pastoral team have made the decision to pursue Alpha, then you should declare your intention to engage in evangelization, identify Alpha as the particular tool you are choosing to use, and inform parishioners that you want all of them to experience it. It isn't difficult to pitch the benefits of Alpha, even for those already in the pews. Alpha is a means to go back to the basics, experience personal growth, and have an increased sense of community with other parishioners. When parishioners participate in Alpha, they familiarize themselves with the tool your parish has chosen for evangelization.

This also means that when it comes time to invite people, you have to lead by example. Whenever I saw someone I didn't know in my parish, the first thing I'd ask them is "Have you tried Alpha?" Ultimately Alpha has to become part of the culture. It's a great challenge to help your parish run Alpha regularly, asking your parishioners to invite an ever-increasing circle of people. But the goal is to weave Alpha so deeply into the fabric of your parish that it's no longer just a program but rather a living reality at the heart of your parish's identity.

Alpha Promotion at Mass

Ron

The two weekends before the start of an Alpha season are key times to promote the event. Here's how Saint Benedict handles it.

At every Mass, the pastor preaches about Alpha in the context of the parish vision. This reminds parishioners of the role that Alpha plays in fulfilling the mission. For the first weekend, the preaching includes an invitation for those *in the parish* who haven't yet taken Alpha. We emphasize that Alpha creates a place where those who already have come to faith can be renewed and enter into an even closer encounter with Christ. We see parishioners who have attended church their entire lives truly encounter Christ for the first time in Alpha.

The subtext here is that many of our parishioners have been sacramentalized, yet we recognize that many of them were never truly evangelized. Therefore we issue this invitation to those already in the pews because we want everyone in our parish to become a disciple of Christ. Even those who have been evangelized benefit from the opportunity to come into a closer relationship with Christ through the Holy Spirit and to experience greater community life. Both weekends before

Alpha starts include a testimony from a lay witness about how Alpha has impacted them.

Our intent during the second weekend is to mobilize parishioners to invite to Alpha those who are disconnected from God or the Church. For the testimony this week, we ask a parishioner to speak about their experience of inviting others or being invited.

This two-weekend period of intentional preaching and witnessing about Alpha before the season launch is essential to continuing and growing an Alpha culture. At Saint Benedict, we've repeated this scenario often enough that it's embedded in the parish culture. Our parishioners expect it. They also expect us to drum away at the need for them to invite people to attend.

It's hard to overstate the case: the ultimate engine that keeps Alpha going and makes it a tool for evangelization is the culture of invitation. In parishes that haven't embraced and strengthened the culture of invitation, Alpha remains little more than a program for churchgoing Christians. It often peaks after two or three years, when 30 to 40 percent of parishioners have taken Alpha. Then the number of attendees sharply drops.

Without a focus on invitation, Alpha will die, and the parish will move on. When this happens, I think the issue is that the parish never truly engaged with Alpha. It takes work to create an invitational focus, but if you get it right, you'll see the percentage of your parishioners participating in Alpha decrease over time while the number of attendees remains the same, as those spots are filled by *unchurched* guests. Those who have already taken Alpha are mobilized to invite those who aren't parishioners. That's what makes the difference between Alpha as a course and Alpha as a culture, a central *tool for evangelization.*

Preparing Testimonies for Mass

It's one thing to talk about Alpha, but it's another thing to hear about Alpha from someone who has actually experienced it. That's why having live testimonies at Mass on the weekends before Alpha is essential.

Before we invite someone to give their testimony at Mass, we ask ourselves if there's any particular demographic we would like to bring to this Alpha. For example, it can be hard to get men to attend. If we specifically want to reach men for an upcoming season, we make sure to schedule at least one man, or often two, to give their testimony at Mass those two weekends. Hearing from another man can help men recognize the positive impact Alpha can have in their lives also.

It's also important to consider the ages of the people giving their testimonies, in terms of the demographic you're trying to reach. When we're hosting a teen group, for example, we ask teens and young adults to offer their testimonies. Also keep in mind that the average age in many congregations is creeping higher as more young people leave. In order to help parishes— and the kingdom—grow, it's important that at least some, if not all, of those giving their testimonies each weekend represent the average age of the surrounding community (younger) rather than that of the parish (older).

Getting the age demographic down for your target audience is valuable, but the most important thing is to select someone who has experienced transformation through Alpha. Once people have agreed to speak, we don't just hope for the best; we help them prepare. We start by asking them to address three points in their testimony:

1. Where were you spiritually before Alpha, and why did you decide to come?
2. What happened to you during Alpha?
3. How has Jesus made a difference in your life since you attended Alpha?

These questions are the foundation for their testimony. After they pull their thoughts together and have their answers, I coach them for success. For example, people tend to give vague answers when I ask what happened during Alpha. I help them drill down to specifics. If they say they made some friends in Alpha, I ask them who they met, how did it feel to make new friends, and what difference have those friendships made for them?

Sometimes people ramble on when covering a particular point. My job as coach is to find the nugget or two that will really resonate with people and then help them craft those into a tight story. I try to help them nail down the essence—the magic—of what happened, so that they can share their story effectively. When it comes to the third question (How has Jesus made a difference in your life since you attended Alpha?) I let them know that it's okay to say that life is still difficult and full of struggles. We want them to be sincere, honest, and real. We don't let them oversell the change that has occurred.

We offer two different presentation options when the time comes for them to share their testimony with the parish. When we know that our speakers are confident, we let them speak for three to four minutes, on their own, from the front of the church, with a prepared text. For those who are less experienced but have a story we want them to share, we do the presentation in an interview style. We stand with them and ask the questions, and they share the specific story we've talked about during their coaching sessions. Doing this together helps them stay on track and, at the same time, helps ease any anxiety they might be feeling. The goal is to set them up for success.

Having people give their testimonies in the weeks leading up to your Alpha season is a huge win and worth the time and effort of all concerned. When relatable people get up and share how Jesus has changed their life, it can help people who are resistant become more open to attending Alpha.

Chapter Nine

The Holy Spirit and Alpha

RON HUNTLEY

I have saved this chapter because, in some measure, it reflects where the Alpha process ultimately leads as we work our way through each season. The Weekend Away, which we will discuss here, is an opportunity for our guests to intentionally open themselves to the Holy Spirit and to their mission as disciples.

The gift of the Holy Spirit is essential to the kerygma, and therefore the Holy Spirit occupies an important place in the Alpha process. The challenge—especially for Catholics who participate in Alpha—is that many of our people do not understand who the Holy Spirit is, and they haven't had an experience of the Holy Spirit's power that they can identify and name. They may view the Holy Spirit as a vague spiritual presence mentioned in the New Testament; they don't expect him to work actively within them or on their behalf. In this worldview, manifestations of the presence and power of the Holy Spirit in the daily lives of ordinary Catholics are seen as strange— even more, as something that we should avoid.

Before we take a look at the Alpha Weekend Away, I think it would help to check in briefly with the Catholic understanding of the Holy Spirit and his involvement in the life of Christians. Right away we see that the Holy Spirit isn't a vague spiritual force but a person—and not only a person but God. The Holy Spirit is the third Person of the Holy Trinity. In the Nicene Creed, we profess that "we believe in the Holy Spirit, the Lord, the giver of life, who proceeds from the Father and the Son." Deacon Keith Strohm, in his book *Jesus: The Story You Thought You Knew*, summarizes the reality of the Holy Spirit like this:

> An encounter with the Holy Spirit is an encounter with God, and the presence of the Holy Spirit within us is the presence of the raw, untamed power of the love of God. Power—that's a good word to use here. Scripture uses that word a lot. Often, the New Testament uses the Greek word for power, *dunamis*. It comes from the same root that we use for words like "dynamite" and "dynamic." When we talk about the presence and power of the Holy Spirit, we are talking about the dynamic, life-changing power of God at work within us and within the world. Jesus himself, after his resurrection, instructed his disciples: "And [behold] I am sending the promise of my Father upon you; but stay in the city until you are clothed with **power** from on high" (Luke 24:49, emphasis mine). . . .
>
> The Lord also promised his Spirit through the prophet Joel, who revealed to the people of Judah the ultimate vindication of the promises of their God when he wrote: "It shall come to pass I will pour out my spirit upon all flesh. Your sons and daughters will prophesy, your old men will dream dreams, your young men will see visions. Even upon your male and female

servants, in those days, I will pour out my spirit" (Joel 3:1–2). In those days, the Spirit rested on just a few: the prophets, the judges of Israel, and the righteous men and women. Here, Joel is prophesying about an outpouring of God's Spirit on all of humanity. When this happens, the Spirit will not only produce fruit *in* us, but also *through* us, for the sake of others.[17]

As Catholics, we believe that we receive the Holy Spirit at Baptism, and the graces received in that experience are sealed in Confirmation. However, the sacraments aren't magic. They require our cooperation. Just because we have received the great gift of the Holy Spirit doesn't mean that we have nothing further to do. It's like receiving a birthday present, for example. I love celebrating my birthday and seeing my gifts piled up in their shiny wrappings. But if I want to truly enjoy those gifts and make them part of my life, I have to actually unwrap them.

It's the same with the gift of the Holy Spirit. There comes a time in our relationship with God when we, as baptized Catholics, must accept the Holy Spirit, whom we have already received, and invite him to be a part of our lives. When we do that, the graces of Baptism and Confirmation are released into our life to an even greater degree. Sometimes this release is accompanied by consolations and a very personal experience of God's love. Other times, we may not experience anything noticeable but over time discover that we possess greater inner freedom, a more acute desire to pray, a deeper understanding of the Bible, more patience, and so on.

The Holy Spirit is not an optional extra in the Christian life. In fact, it is the Holy Spirit who makes it possible for us to live as disciples of Jesus Christ, who empowers us to grow in holiness and help transform the lives of others. That's why the Alpha process carves out special time, called the Weekend Away, to help both the unchurched and guests who are baptized encounter the presence and power of the Holy Spirit.

The Weekend Away

We have discovered, in running Alpha over the years, that the Weekend Away is the turning point for many guests. The fellowship, food, discussion, and teaching experienced in the previous six Alpha evenings help guests open their hearts to the possibility of God's love and care for them. The weekend experience makes that love present to them in tangible ways. Two things often happen on the Weekend Away: lives are transformed, and relationships move to a deeper level.

That's why we prioritize holding a Weekend Away for every Alpha. We tell our guests about the Weekend Away up front without making a big deal of it. During Week 2 we mention it briefly, but we only start pressing for commitments after Week 3. Relationships are forming and our guests are more comfortable and engaged.

We know that people are busy. Many have family obligations, often both spouses have jobs, and their kids can be in a variety of activities. We could extend our Alpha sessions and show the Holy Spirit-focused videos sequentially over a series of weeks, but we would miss out on the impact of the Weekend Away. This weekend experience not only focuses on the person and activity of the Holy Spirit, but it helps guests reflect on their lives and make room for the Holy Spirit. We do offer a Holy Spirit Day—an "in-town" experience as part of the daytime Alpha as mentioned in chapter 6—but we don't offer it as an option up front, preferring instead to emphasize the importance of the weekend event. Even though the Weekend Away takes more time to plan and costs money, in our experience, that investment bears much fruit.

Weekend Away Schedule

Let's take a look at our current Weekend Away schedule, followed by a short description of the various elements. This schedule has changed over time and will undoubtedly change again, but this is what works best for us right now.

Day 1
  11:00 a.m. – Arrival, Check-In
  11:30 a.m. – Welcome and Introduction
  12:00 p.m. – Lunch
  1:00 p.m. – First Talk
  1:45 p.m. – Free Time
  3:45 p.m. – Second Talk
  4:30 p.m. – Small Group
  5:15 p.m. – Break
  5:45 p.m. – Third Talk
  6:20 p.m. – Ministry Time
  7:00 p.m. – Dinner
  8:00 p.m. – Skits and Fun

Day 2
  8:00 a.m. – Breakfast
  9:00 a.m. – Fourth Talk

9:45 a.m. – Small Group
10:30 a.m. – Group Sharing
11:15 a.m. – Wrap-Up

As people gather the first morning, our music ministry plays songs to set the mood and build a sense of excitement for the weekend. Once everyone is settled, we give a ten-minute welcome. We've put padding in the schedule here, to give people time to unwind, get comfortable, and maybe introduce themselves to people they don't know: we'll have guests from all our satellite Alphas and sometimes we invite guests from other churches that are running Alpha to join us.

After lunch, at around 1:00, we open with a couple of praise and worship songs and then have our first talk. (Alpha provides videos for these talks, but you can also do them live.) We follow this with a lengthy break, which allows our guests to explore the grounds, unwind, journal, or connect with their friends. We want people to have time to decompress from their busy week and make room in their minds and hearts for God.

We sing more praise-and-worship songs as we regroup for the second talk. After the talk, we gather for small-group discussion, followed by a break and snacks. During this break, we call together our prayer ministry teams (more on this in a moment) and show each team where they will be stationed for ministry after the next talk. That third talk takes place at 5:45 p.m.

When the prayer ministry time comes to a close, following the third talk, we ask everyone to go back to their tables for dinner and to plan their skits. For many, the prayer ministry time will have been powerful and emotional, so planning a skit gives everyone a chance to relax and get silly. The rest of the evening is devoted to fun: we put on our skits, pull out guitars, sing campfire songs, and encourage people to play games together.

The next morning starts with breakfast, followed by praise and worship and our final talk. After one last small group session, we give people an opportunity to share how God has worked in their hearts during the weekend. Following these often powerful testimonies, we conclude with a short wrap-up and see our guests out as they head home for lunch.

Prayer Ministry on the Weekend Away

Many Catholics aren't familiar with the term "prayer ministry." It simply means setting aside time to pray with an individual or group of people. It's an important part of the Alpha experience, and Alpha provides general guidelines on how to go about praying with others.

During the Weekend Away, prayer ministry occurs on Saturday evening, after the talk entitled "How Can I Be Filled with the Holy Spirit?" We move from that talk into a period of prayer with our guests, asking the Lord to fill them with the Holy Spirit. Remember, for the baptized, who have already received the Holy Spirit, this is a prayer of release so that they can open themselves more deliberately to the grace of the sacraments. For the unbaptized, we pray that the Father will reveal his love to them in Jesus through the power of the Holy Spirit.

This can be a transformative time for our guests. For some, it offers the first tangible experience of God's love that they've ever had.

Here is how we structure the prayer ministry time. After the video or live talk, we start the general (corporate) prayer ministry time by asking our guests if they want to be filled with the Holy Spirit. We invite them to stand and open their hands in a receptive prayer posture as we call on the Holy Spirit in prayer. We all pray the Come, Holy Spirit prayer. During this time, we make room for silence.

The emcee leads this prayer time, and the music ministry offers general support. When we're ready to transition from corporate prayer ministry to personal prayer ministry, the emcee gives instructions about the logistics and cues the musicians to play reflective instrumental music. While the Alpha team is praying with individuals, we ask everyone to remain in prayer and to avoid the temptation to chat.

Here's how the actual prayer ministry unfolds. Prayer teams, made up of two Alpha team members of the same gender, are stationed around the room. Prior to the weekend, we make sure we have enough prayer teams for the number of guests. Because we have men pray with men and women with women, we make sure that we have the correct ratio of male and female teams based on the guests attending. If we have a higher proportion of female guests, for example, we make sure to have a higher proportion of female prayer teams. One of the team members will have experience praying with others, and one may be new to the role.

Before prayer begins, the emcee reminds the guests about the prayer gesture known as the laying on of hands. The preceding talk—"How Can I Be Filled with the Holy Spirit?"—speaks about the scriptural precedent for this gesture, which simply involves placing a hand on the shoulder of the person with whom we are praying. We invite our guests to go to a team of their gender for prayer. The team members ask permission to place a hand gently on the guest's shoulder and will do so if given permission. They ask the guest if they want prayer for anything specific, and if so, the team prays for that intention and more generally for a release of the presence and power of the Holy Spirit. When most of the people who stepped forward for prayer have been taken care of, the emcee extends another invitation. Often the second invitation leads to an influx of people who initially held back.

Of course, there are other ways to approach the prayer time. I am aware of Alpha teams, for example, who encourage members of the small groups to sit together for the talk. As the talk concludes and the emcee prays and asks the Holy Spirit to come, they then wait in a period of silence. After a short time, the host and helpers team up and one by one go to the members of their small group and simply ask if they can pray for them. Because small group members already have a relationship with their host and helpers, this can be a natural and organic way for the prayer time to proceed.

After the individual prayer time is complete, we re-enter corporate prayer through more praise-and-worship music. The music team leads a song with a repetitive chorus, and the emcee invites our guests to enter into a posture of prayer. We then invite everyone to speak out their spontaneous praise to God. Letting gratitude and praise well up inside us and then speaking it out loud to God can be a powerful experience, especially for those who haven't done this before. We know that culturally, Catholics are not always comfortable with this, but we have seen the Lord work powerfully in people's hearts when they surrender enough to pray in this way.

The time of spontaneous praise doesn't last long, maybe a minute or so, but it can be transforming. It offers our guests an opportunity to encounter the Holy Spirit in more than an intellectual or theological way.

After the time of spontaneous praise, we invite our guests to further their encounter with the Holy Spirit by singing in tongues. First, we encourage them to be open to this gift and then we lead by example, saying "Alleluia" over and over and allowing different sounds to rise up naturally. This too only lasts for a minute or so. We close the prayer time by finishing the song and then we bless the meal and have dinner.

Getting Comfortable with Prayer Ministry

Many parishes have trouble teaching their Alpha teams how to cooperate with the Holy Spirit as they pray with guests. I understand that not everyone is at ease praying with others or with the manifestations and gifts of the Holy Spirit—I wasn't when I started running Alpha. However, as we prayed with guests, I could see that they were being moved and were experiencing the presence of God. I finally accepted the fact that my comfort level isn't the final measure of what God can accomplish in and through me. Cooperating with the Holy Spirit requires us to surrender and take risks. It calls us to have faith. We may be uncomfortable, but that shouldn't prevent us from expecting great things of the Spirit. If we live in his power, we can help others do so too.

In order to give team members confidence and keep newly acquired prayer skills fresh in their minds, we train our prayer teams for this ministry the week before we go on the Weekend

Away. Our prayer teams already know each other because they've been part of the Alpha season in various roles and have built up cohesion and camaraderie. To deepen that, we begin our training with a time for socializing. After that, we watch a video produced by Alpha International about how to pray with others, and then we practice by praying over each other—real-time prayer, not go-through-the-motions prayer.

This is where the rubber hits the road.

Every time we do this, people want to run for their lives when they realize that they're actually going to pray over each other *right then and there*. The first time Fr. James and I ran Alpha at Saint Benedict, we decided to start big. We had plenty of Alpha experience elsewhere and believed that together we could pull it off. (We often recommend starting small and then scaling up from there, but with our combined experience, we decided to take the risk.) The upshot was that about 80 percent of our team had never done Alpha before. When it came time to train them for prayer ministry, we told them how we pray with guests, showed them the Alpha video, and said that after a short break, we would come back to pray over each other in the way we'd just seen in the Alpha video.

During the break, several people told me that they were uncomfortable and reluctant to follow through. One woman in particular was really stressed out. I could see her husband pacing back and forth at the back of the room as she told me that they had to leave because they felt they couldn't do it. I told her that I would never have invited her to do something I felt she couldn't do. I encouraged and reassured her, saying it would be all right if she gave it a try. I shared the same thing with her husband, and they agreed to participate.

That simple act of trying, even though they were uncomfortable, changed their lives. They served on Alpha with us for several years and are two of our most steadfast Connect Group leaders. They now love praying with people.

When Fr. James first ran Alpha in his first parish, he knew that most of his parishioners would be uncomfortable serving in prayer ministry, and so for the Weekend Away, he brought in what he called the "prayer experts." They prayed with people on the weekend, and it went great. The problem was, when the guests from that weekend came back to serve on an Alpha team, they weren't willing to pray with people. They insisted that Father bring back the prayer experts. The new team members were convinced they couldn't do what those prayer experts had done, with all their eloquence and grace. Fr. James said it was a mistake to bring in the "experts," one he never repeated. We want to approach prayer ministry in Alpha in such a simple manner that everyone can do it.

In fact, over time we train the entire Alpha team—including those who serve in operations and the kitchen—to pray with other people. We want all of them to learn these principles because if they can become relaxed about praying with people, then maybe they can do it at home, at work, or wherever they are. If we learn how to pray *with* people and not just *for* people, we can more effectively be channels of God's love and healing to others.

Training Tips

First things first: it might sound too minor to even mention, but we ask our prayer ministry teams to smile as people approach seeking prayer. If you're praying with people for the first time, you're probably terrified—smiling might be the last thing on your mind. But the people coming up to receive prayer are also scared and uncertain, and that smile can set them at ease and increase their receptivity.

For training purposes, we group people into teams of three, led by someone who has prayed over people before or who might be more comfortable or, should I say, is not as scared. We partner that person with two less experienced team members. I make sure that we don't group friends with friends. I've noticed that when friends get together in a team, they're less likely to do what we've asked—engage in real prayer—and more likely to fake it by just going through the motions.

We designate the more experienced person to lead the prayer, one person to receive prayer, and the third person to pray in support of the leader. In other words, we have them practice according to the model we use on the Weekend Away. The person leading the prayer says to the person they are praying for, "How can we pray for you today?" and "Is there anything else?" The team member being prayed for names some requests and then the leader invites the team member to close their eyes and enter into a posture of receptive prayer. The leader and support person, however, keep their eyes open while praying in order to keep watch over what's happening with the person being prayed for.

The prayer leader asks permission to lay hands on the person in prayer. Also, because there are moments of silence during prayer ministry, the leader says that they will let the prayer recipient know when the prayer time is over.

The leader brings the prayer requests to the Lord and prays for a release of the Holy Spirit in the life of the person with whom they are praying. The support person, in turn, tries to listen for what the Holy Spirit might have for the prayer recipient and can add a word of prayer when appropriate. If the person leading prayer gives the support person the opportunity to share, we ask the support person to be brief and not contradict what the leader has already said. On the Alpha weekend, we often have prayer ministers take turns leading and supporting.

After we've practiced praying over one another in teams, I gather everyone back together and ask them how it went. Usually most of the team admit that they weren't sure going into it that they had anything to bring to the table. After the experience, most of them are filled with joy and surprised by what happened—we're actually praying over people, and so things happen. This may seem a bit wild, but we have seen healings and miracles in our training sessions (and during Alpha too).

It's moving to hear people's feedback after praying over their fellow team members; it builds up everyone in the room. Training is more than passing on a skill. Teaching people to pray over each other helps them grow in their faith and leadership simultaneously. They witness the power of God right before their eyes.

Please don't go halfway with your Alpha training in this area, giving in to the temptation to let your teams fake it. And don't bring in "prayer experts" during prayer ministry sessions. Engage your team in praying over each other, encourage them to see past their very natural fears, and you'll find that your investment will bear rich fruit in their lives and in the culture of your parish.

Chapter 10

Does God Heal Today?

RON HUNTLEY

In addition to the Weekend Away, there is another Alpha session where we offer prayer ministry for our guests. This takes place during Week 9, the evening devoted to the question "Does God Heal Today?" We believe the answer to that question is *yes*. I think we can agree that much of the healing done today is at the hands of doctors with the help of medicine and medical procedures. Our understanding of science has added twenty years to the average life span in the West since the end of World War II. I believe that this is the healing work of God. In fact, the hospital system is one of the great legacies of Christianity. From the beginning, the Catholic Church has established hospitals as a response to suffering, and priests, nuns, and laity alike have ministered there to the sick and dying.

I suppose the second part of that question, however, is this: Does God still heal miraculously today as he did in the Bible? And if we take that a step further, can he use you and me, moved with compassion, to pray for healing for others? And if we did, would anyone be healed?

The Bible makes it pretty clear that praying for healing is part of the ongoing work of following Jesus. He tells his disciples to "make this proclamation: 'The kingdom of heaven is at hand. Cure the sick, raise the dead, cleanse lepers, drive out demons. Without cost you have received; without cost you are to give'" (Matthew 10:6-8). After Jesus rose from the dead, he confirmed this ministry, telling his disciples not only to "go into the whole world and proclaim the gospel," but also that "they will lay hands on the sick, and they will recover" (Mark 16:15, 18).

Personal Experience

As a cradle Catholic, I grew up praying with my mom for relatives and friends who were sick. I was genuinely concerned for these sick friends and relatives, and I prayed for them the only way I knew how, through rote prayer or the Rosary and such. No one had ever taught me to lay hands on them and pray for healing directly. Such prayer seems far more intimate and caring, but I didn't know it was possible.

Through my participation in Alpha I have learned to pray more, to pray out loud with others, to pray for healing with others, and to ask for others to pray with me for healing. Has it worked? Let me share my first-hand experience.

Like many men, when I have a medical issue I don't go to the doctor. Why? Because the problem will go away, right? Well, not always. When I was in my late twenties, I developed a wart on my foot. It didn't go away—in fact it spread to both feet and multiplied. I was embarrassed, but after years of ignoring it I went to the doctor. Upon examination he said,

"This is the worst case of plantar warts I have ever seen." Great! That began years of aggressive and painful treatment that didn't work. Every few months the doctor would burn them off, and the treatment would leave the bottoms of my feet swollen and painful. (Have I sufficiently grossed you out yet? Sorry about that.)

One day, a friend who had learned about my "issue" nonchalantly asked if I'd ever had anyone pray over my feet. I thought to myself, "What a ridiculous thing to ask. As if prayer could make a difference." I didn't want to expose my disbelief, however, so I pretended that it was a perfectly reasonable question and simply responded, "No, I haven't." She asked if I would let her say a prayer. "That seems bizarre," I thought to myself, but she cared about me and thought this would help. I figured if nothing else it might make her feel better. I said, "Sure."

She prayed, "Lord, please heal the warts on Ron's feet fully, completely, and may they never return. In the name of Jesus I pray. Amen." I thought to myself, "I have been receiving aggressive and painful medical treatment and you think that simple prayer is going to work? You are out of your mind!" I just said, "Thank you."

A couple of days later my friend asked me how my feet were. I was so used to the issue that I said they were fine. She asked if I had checked to see if the warts were gone and when I said no, she said, "Check right now."

I thought, "This is silly but to show you that your simple prayer was useless, I will look." I took off my shoe and sock and looked. I didn't say a word but quickly took off my other shoe and sock and stared, dumbfounded. My friend asked, "Are they gone?"

"Yes, totally gone." Neither foot showed a trace that I had ever had a problem. Do you know what? The warts have never returned. It was a miracle. A simple prayer of faith from a Catholic believer to a skeptical hypocrite. The healing had nothing to do with my faith—I had none. Since then, people have prayed with me and I have received healing for chronic tendinitis, neck and shoulder pain, and many other things. I can tell you for sure that I have received healing at the hands of prayer and in the name of Jesus.

What do you think that has done for my understanding of how God wants to work through others, as Jesus said? Do I still have a doctor? Of course! Doctors, medicine, and procedures are the main way God is bringing healing and relief to those who are suffering.

Have I ever prayed with anyone whom God then healed? Yes. I remember praying with a friend named Pia who was from Columbia and was pregnant. She developed a lump behind her ear and was very scared. It was aggressive, she didn't know what it was, she hadn't seen her doctor yet, and she was worried that whatever it was might affect her baby. I asked if I could pray with her for healing. She agreed. Here's how I prayed: "Lord, thank you for Pia. She is scared and we need your help. Please take away this bump in the name of Jesus. Amen." Simple and not weird, right? We hugged, she thanked me, and then she checked it. It was instantly and totally gone. Both of us were shocked and we hugged again as she cried and we both gave thanks. What do you think that did for our faith?

A God Who Heals

On our night during Alpha when we focus on healing, God has healed people of chronic psoriasis, chronic pain, chronic numbness, restricted motion, and migraines. He has also instantly healed addictions to alcohol and smoking, and he has done much more as well. There have been as many (or more) spiritual healings as there have been physical healings. Many have received healing who asked for help forgiving others for abuse of many kinds, hurtful work situations, anger, jealousy, broken relationships, and the like.

Does God heal everyone? No, not in our experience. But when we didn't pray for healing, no one was healed. When we started to do what Jesus commanded and began praying for God to heal people in the name of Jesus, some were healed. That has increased the faith of many of those who witness it first-hand and know the people who testify about what God has done for them. Jesus is still in the healing business. The question is, are we still in the praying-for-miracles business? If not, why not give God another chance? For that to happen, we must get out of our heads, break through the fear, and dare to do what Jesus taught us, not worrying about the outcome.

God does want to use us to pray with those around us, keeping in mind that he does the healing, not us. God parted the sea, not Moses. But God refused to do it until Moses raised his staff. Why? I don't know. Maybe it is because God wants to bring about his plan of salvation with us. He is a team player and often invites us to play our very small part because he loves us.

Some Points for the Session

Here are a few practical tips to make the ministry time for Week 9 a bit more comfortable. The more you prayerfully prepare for this special session, the greater probability it has of bearing "fruit that will remain" (John 15:16). I only ask that you resist the temptation to chicken out because of fear. Even now, when I am emcee for this session, my temptation is to chicken out because I know I can't heal anyone, no one on the team can heal anyone, and we will all be embarrassed if God doesn't show up. We wrestle with this each time—and we do it anyway. We do it in faith. We do it in obedience. And we invite you to do the same.

Preparing Your Team

Most people on your Alpha team will have experienced the healing session when they went through Alpha as a guest. They're aware of the general flow of the evening. At the follow-up team meeting after Week 8, remind them that next week the talk and the prayer will center on healing.

To that end, encourage people to pray during the week, asking the Lord to show them the healing he wants to offer the Alpha guests. Sometimes, the Holy Spirit can plant wisdom in our hearts about who and how he wants to heal. He can send us images, sympathy pains, or a strong conviction that he wants to bring healing to a specific illness or dysfunction. These promptings have been called words of knowledge, and they are mentioned by St. Paul in his list of spiritual gifts found in 1 Corinthians 12:4-11.

In regard to this, however, it's important for team members to understand what words of knowledge are *not*.

When you know someone in your Alpha course has a specific health issue, that is human knowledge, not the spiritual gift of knowledge. We leave plenty of room in the ministry time for guests to bring forward their own issues and receive prayer—they don't need to wait for a specific word that might not come. Further, we instruct everyone to respect the privacy of others and not bring up another person's struggles if they happen to know about them.

And finally, we are not fishing. What I mean is that we are not throwing out generic issues that have a high probability of drawing a response from a large group of people. We are asking God to let us know what *he* wants to heal, and we are listening to him. This is not a science. We don't always get it right, and yet we have never done a healing night where someone was not miraculously healed.

If I can put it in simple terms, words of knowledge occur when God reveals something to you that you would otherwise know nothing about. I know, it sounds supernatural. It is! But it isn't weird. I experience it as a very gentle prompting, and it requires that I take a risk and give voice to it. I am not saying I receive something every time, but when I ask and listen I sometimes do.

Have your Alpha team members pray and ask God to help them be open to those words of knowledge. Instruct them to write down any promptings they receive when they ask God who he wants to heal that week. The next week, in the pre-meeting for the healing night, team members will hand in those words of knowledge. Sometimes there are more words than there is ministry time, so I thank people for participating in this prayer exercise and ask them to trust my discernment. Many team members share how they were impacted during the week as they prayed to God, asking him to reveal what he was going to heal. Since this is not something many people often do, it can have a tremendous impact on their relationship with God and their ability to trust him.

Praying with People

If you are the emcee, lean into prayer that week. I recommend going to the Sacrament of Reconciliation if possible. God's healing hand does not depend on your holiness, yet at the same time, it's good to be free of sin while leading others in this ministry time. The emcee is simply being obedient to the commands of Jesus, trusting in the prayers and discernment of the team, and creating a space for God to work. It is God who will do the work.

As on the Weekend Away, the emcee will need to let guests know that after the talk (or video), there will be time for prayer ministry before heading to small groups. When the talk is over, we invite our guests to stand for the prayer time, and we explain that the team has been praying and asking God for words of knowledge regarding specific healings. We will read those out loud and pray as the prayer time unfolds.

We ask everyone to keep their eyes closed, and as the emcee reads out the words of knowledge from the team members, we invite anyone in the room who feels that these words might be for them to raise their hand. Team members will go over to them and pray that God will heal them. I have been constantly surprised by the specificity of the promptings that the Holy Spirit has given to our team.

Once this time of prayer is finished, let people know they can bring forward anything they would like prayer for in their small groups and release them to pray with each other in those groups.

As with all things Alpha, we resist intensity and weirdness. Keep the healing session simple, light, and to the point. Have fun, and please consider dropping me a line with your stories of healing at ron@divinerenovation.net.

Chapter Eleven

Concluding Thoughts

RON HUNTLEY AND FR. JAMES MALLON

Ron

At the end of the day, Jesus is going to ask each of us, "How have you loved me, loved others, and built up the kingdom of God?" I want to have the right answer.

For many years, Catholics have heard that we are called to be part of the New Evangelization. I'm sure many of you, like me, have wondered how to put that call into action. Often we haven't seemed to have the tools we need to reach those who have fallen away from the Church and those who have yet to encounter Christ. At Saint Benedict, we discovered the means to put that evangelistic call into action when we encountered Alpha. Fr. James and I can say that in our many years of working to bring people to Jesus, Alpha has turned out to be the most effective tool we have found.

Since we started running Alpha in January 2011, approximately two thousand people have tried Alpha with us, and that number grows every year. Running Alpha has been the catalyst for the transformation of the entire parish. We have seen both faithful and indifferent Catholics experience powerful conversions and come alive in Jesus Christ. We have seen the unchurched, many of whom never gave Jesus or Christianity a second thought, begin a relationship with him and become engaged, passionate members of our parish. We are now seeing entire families come to faith. Each year at our Easter Vigil, we welcome more and more Alpha graduates into full communion with the Church. Saint Benedict Parish has started to move from maintenance to mission! Alpha is an important part of making that happen.

When you run Alpha well in your parish, you are going to reach those who already sit in the pews and those outside the Church—and Jesus is going to change their lives. Every season, when someone stands before the congregation and testifies to what Alpha has done for them, you are going to look out over that congregation and see that this change doesn't belong just to that person but to everyone in your community. This is what the New Evangelization can look like. This isn't about saving buildings from closing; it's about building up the body of Christ and welcoming home those who are lost.

Alpha came into my life as an unexpected and unasked-for gift, and it quickly transformed everything I knew about evangelization. It became the answer to the questions I had regarding how we could bring people to Jesus and to the Catholic Church, which I have loved since my youth. I wrote this book because I want to pass that same gift on to you, including information that will help you use Alpha as effectively as possible in your parish. I hope you've found inspiration here, as well as practical advice on how to avoid certain pitfalls and maximize the effectiveness of Alpha. My prayer is that as you tap into the vast resources of the Alpha organization, reflect on the advice in this book, and explore the Divine Renovation resources for parish renewal in the appendix, you will see the fruits of Alpha in the lives of your people and the culture of your parish from the very first season.

We have learned from our victories and challenges over our years of running Alpha, but this book isn't meant to be the final word on how Alpha can work in a Catholic context. I hope it will serve as a guide but also as a springboard, encouraging you to innovate according to your specific situation. You are not alone. There are online tools and videos available at run.alpha.org to support you and your team, and there are also live training events and Alpha coaches who can help you. Be patient as you implement Alpha and as you learn how best to use it in your parish. As you engage your staff and parishioners, you will find that Alpha can be a powerful tool to help you in the mission of bringing people to Christ and forming them as leaders.

A Bountiful Harvest

Fr. James

Introducing others to Jesus is the grounding passion of my life.

But as most pastors know, it's easy to get caught up in the administrative tasks of running a parish and, in many churches, overwhelmed by the demands of maintaining the health of a community that is demonstrably growing smaller. As our seminaries form fewer and fewer priests, the formation there can contribute to this maintenance-oriented pastoral approach by emphasizing therapeutic pastoral care over forming disciples.

But as the world has shifted away from faith, many of our people—let alone the unchurched and the fallen away—need a different sort of leadership from their priests, one that leads them into an intimate relationship with Jesus.

Once people are set on fire with the love of Jesus and empowered by the Holy Spirit, they will be equipped to share the good news in word and deed. This is what the world needs—not Christians locked away in their parish communities, chiefly focused on taking inventory and wondering how long they'll be able to keep their buildings open. The Alpha experience can help parishes bring their people to that sort of transformation.

The dominant culture is either indifferent or hostile to what we believe. In response, some within the Church suggest we build ever higher walls around us and only admit people who sound like us. Engaging with people outside our walls is seen as a betrayal and an accommodation of the truth. Yet God himself pitched his tent among us and met us where we were—in the midst of our rebellion—in order to bring us home.

We must do the same.

We need both great theology and a great model for how to live out our faith. Great theology—of which we have an abundance—isn't worth much if it has no way to impact the lives of people. And the best model of how to live out our Catholic faith cannot produce lasting fruit if it is not grounded in the truth. In the course of our history as Catholics, we have had amazing theology without a lived model, and we have had models of lived faith without much theology. Used well, Alpha can provide the foundation of a lived model of parish life that allows us, ultimately, to express fully the reality of mission and discipleship to which we are called by Christ. It can serve as the core of a larger engine of evangelization that produces lasting fruit.

Ever since my first encounter with Alpha in 2000, I have been open to finding a better tool. I haven't found one yet. Throughout that time, I have witnessed the power of God transforming the unlikeliest of people and bringing forth life in the most barren situations—on a regular basis. It's no lie to say that Alpha has changed my experience of the priesthood. I'm positive that whether you are ordained or a layperson, once you see people come alive in Jesus through the power of the Holy Spirit, you'll never be satisfied with sending people through programs that have little impact.

My prayer is that this book has helped awaken a hunger in your heart to see this kind of transformation at your parish. Ultimately it isn't about supporting Alpha or running this specific program; it's about shifting your culture and the hearts of your people to embrace the mission of Christ and make disciples of everyone they encounter.

I wish you a bountiful harvest!

Endnotes

1. Fr. James Mallon, *Divine Renovation: Bringing Your Parish from Maintenance to Mission* (New London, CT: Twenty-Third Publications, 2014), 21.
2. Pew Research Center, "Religious Landscape Study," 2015, http://www.pewresearch.org/fact-tank/2015/09/15/half-of-u-s-adults-raised-catholic-have-left-the-church-at-some-point.
3. Pope Francis, *Evangelii Gaudium* [The Joy of the Gospel], November 24, 2013, no. 27, http://w2.vatican.va/content/francesco/en/apost_exhortations/documents/papa-francesco_esortazione-ap_20131124_evangelii-gaudium.html.
4. Kevin Kruse, Stephen Covey: 10 Quotes That Can Change Your Life, https://www.forbes.com/sites/kevinkruse/2012/07/16/the-7-habits/#669baf5039c6
5. Pope Benedict XVI, *Deus Caritas Est* [God Is Love], December 25, 2005, no. 1, http://w2.vatican.va/content/benedict-xvi/en/encyclicals/documents/hf_ben-xvi_enc_20051225_deus-caritas-est.html.
6. Pope John Paul II, quoted in *L'Osservatore Romano*, January 14, 1991, no. 2.
7. Pope Paul VI, *Evangelii Nuntiandi*, [Evangelization in the Modern World], December 8, 1975, no. 14, http://w2.vatican.va/content/paul-vi/en/apost_exhortations/documents/hf_p-vi_exh_19751208_evangelii-nuntiandi.html.
8. Pope John Paul II, *Catechesi Tradendae*, [Catechesis in Our Time], October 16, 1979, no. 25, http://w2.vatican.va/content/john-paul-ii/en/apost_exhortations/documents/hf_jp-ii_exh_16101979_catechesi-tradendae.html.
9. Mallon, 142.

10. Pope John Paul II, *Catechesi Tradendae*, no. 5.

11. Congregation for the Clergy, *General Directory for Catechesis*, 1997, no. 47, quoting Vatican II, *Ad Gentes*, [Decree on the Mission Activity of the Church], no. 6, http://www.vatican.va/roman_curia/congregations/cclergy/documents/rc_con_ccatheduc_doc_17041998_directory-for-catechesis_en.html.

12. Pope Francis, *Evangelii Gaudium*, no. 164.

13. Pope Paul VI, *Lumen Gentium* [Dogmatic Constitution on the Church], November 21, 1964, no. 26, http://www.vatican.va/archive/hist_councils/ii_vatican_council/documents/vat-ii_const_19641121_lumen-gentium_en.html.

14. Pew Research Center, "Religious Landscape Survey," 2018, http://www.pewforum.org/2018/04/25/when-americans-say-they-believe-in-god-what-do-they-mean/.

15. United States Conference of Catholic Bishops, *Go and Make Disciples: A National Plan and Strategy for Catholic Evangelization in the United States* (Washington: USCCB, 2002), 10, http://www.usccb.org/beliefs-and-teachings/how-we-teach/evangelization/go-and-make-disciples/what_is_evangelization_go_and_make_disciples.cfm.

16. Ralph Nader, as quoted in Tanya Prive, "Top 32 Quotes Every Entrepreneur Should Live By," www.forbes.com/sites/tanyaprive/2013/05/02/top-32-quotes-every-entrepreneur-should-live-by/#36fdf7de19a9, May 2, 2013.

17. Keith Strohm, *Jesus: The Story You Thought You Knew* (Huntington, IN: Our Sunday Visitor, 2017), 132.

Divine Renovation Ministry

Are you and your parish ready to move from maintenance to mission?

You don't need to journey alone. The Divine Renovation Ministry coaches pastors and leadership teams as they take their parish from maintenance to mission. Visit www. divinerenovation.net to connect with the ministry and start the process of making joyful missionary disciples.

www.DivineRenovation.net

Divine Renovation Resources

Mallon, Fr. James. *Divine Renovation: Bringing Your Parish from Maintenance to Mission*. New London, CT: Twenty-Third Publications, 2014.

————. *Divine Renovation Guidebook: A Step-by-Step Manual for Transforming Your Parish*. New London, CT: Twenty-Third Publications, 2016.

Lobo, Fr. Simon, CC. *Divine Renovation Apprentice: Learning to Lead a Disciple-Making Parish*. Frederick, MD: The Word Among Us Press, 2018.

Ready to begin the journey?
Find out how Alpha is more than a curriculum.

Step 1: What are these talks all about?

Watch any and all the Alpha talks at **alphausa.org/watch** or **alphacanada.org/try** or **run.alpha.org.uk**

Step 2: Connect with Alpha Locally.

We have Alpha staff and church leaders who would love to talk to you and answer questions you may have. Visit **alphausa.org/contact** or **alphacanada.org/connect** or **alpha.org.uk/contact**

STEP 3: Get Started.

Log on to **run.alpha.org** to register your Alpha and download all the resources you need to train, plan and promote your Alpha.

Printed promotional materials can be found online, or if in the USA, you can contact **print.alpharesources.org.**

All of the Alpha resources can be found at the Alpha's resources store: **ChurchSource.com/Alpha** and if in Canada, you can order via **Amazon.ca**. If in the UK please visit **shop.alpha.org** for promotional materials and all Alpha resources.

The Run Alpha Kit

The *Run Alpha Kit* will help you to plan, promote, and run your first Alpha. It includes two DVD options, *Alpha Guide, Alpha Team Guide, Run Alpha Handbook*, which is essential for every Alpha administrator, and copies of *Why Jesus?*, *Why Easter?* and *Why Christmas?* booklets. (US and Canada only)

Alpha Film Series

The *Alpha Film Series* is emotive, engaging and epic in scale and scope. Nicky Gumbel and two new presenters, Toby Flint and Gemma Hunt, walk through the basics of the Christian faith in a way that everyone can relate to. Repackaged for today's audience, the episodes feature inspiring stories and interviews from all around the world. The DVD includes fifteen episodes (30 minutes each), and two required team training sessions on how to lead an Alpha small group.

Alpha Guide

The *Alpha Guide* is a companion to either the *Alpha Film Series* or *Alpha with Nicky Gumbel* DVD. This guide is divided up by session with an easy-to-read outline so that guests can follow along during each talk. With simple bullet-point organization and plenty of room for notes, it is considered an essential resource for Alpha guests as well as the host and helpers on Alpha.

Alpha Team Guide

The *Alpha Team Guide* is recommended for Alpha small group hosts and helpers. It includes notes for the two required team training sessions on how to lead an Alpha small group, and how to lead prayer ministry. It also provides weekly key concept summary and suggested questions to help guide the discussion time for each session of Alpha.

Run Alpha Handbook

For Alpha directors and leaders, this is one of the most important tools in setting up and running an Alpha. This essential how-to resource offers a guided tour through every stage of setting up and running your Alpha, including reproducible resources to make it easy to recruit and train your Alpha team. (US and Canada only)

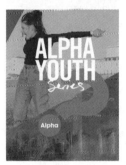

Alpha Youth Series DVD and Discussion Guide Pack

The main thing you will notice about Alpha is the quality. We believe the Church—and the Gospel—deserve the highest quality and we want your group to be proud to invite their friends to Alpha. The Alpha Youth Series is designed for 13- to 18-year-olds. Each episode will include discussion breaks for conversation, and personal testimonies related to the theme.

Alpha USA
1635 Emerson Lane
Naperville, IL 60540
questions@alphausa.org
800.362.5742
alphausa.org
@alphausa

Alpha Canada
101 – 26 Fourth St.
New Westminster, BC
V3L 5M4
office@alphacanada.org
800.743.0899
alphacanada.org
@alphacanada

Alpha in the Caribbean
Holy Trinity Brompton
Brompton Road
London SW7 1JA
United Kingdom
americas@alpha.org
44 (0) 845.644.7544
caribbean.alpha.org
@AlphaCaribbean

Alpha UK
Holy Trinity Brompton
Brompton Road
London, SW7 1JA
United Kingdom
uk@alpha.org
44 (0) 207.052.0200
alpha.org.uk
@alphacourseuk

Based somewhere else?

Alpha has offices all around the world. Find your local office at **alpha.org/global** or visit our global website **alpha.org.**

the WORD
among us ®
The *Spirit* of Catholic Living

This book was published by The Word Among Us. Since 1981, The Word Among Us has been answering the call of the Second Vatican Council to help Catholic laypeople encounter Christ in the Scriptures.

The name of our company comes from the prologue to the Gospel of John and reflects the vision and purpose of all of our publications: to be an instrument of the Spirit, whose desire is to manifest Jesus' presence in and to the children of God. In this way, we hope to contribute to the Church's ongoing mission of proclaiming the gospel to the world so that all people would know the love and mercy of our Lord and grow more deeply in their faith as missionary disciples.

Our monthly devotional magazine, *The Word Among Us*, features meditations on the daily and Sunday Mass readings, and currently reaches more than one million Catholics in North America and another half million Catholics in one hundred countries around the world. Our book division, The Word Among Us Press, publishes numerous books, Bible studies, and pamphlets that help Catholics grow in their faith.

To learn more about who we are and what we publish, visit us at www.wau.org. There you will find a variety of Catholic resources that will help you grow in your faith.

Embrace His Word, Listen to God . . .

www.wau.org